T0325304

AN ERA
—OF THE—
WISE MAN

www.royalcollins.com

AN ERA
—OF THE—
WISE MAN
THE EXPECTATION-LED
MARKET PRINCIPLE

Ruyu Zhao

Books Beyond Boundaries

ROYAL COLLINS

An Era of The Wise Man: The Expectation-Led Market Principle

Ruyu Zhao

© Ruyu Zhao
First published in 2021 by Royal Collins Publishing Group Inc.
Groupe Publication Royal Collins Inc.
BKM Royalcollins Publishers Private Limited

Headquarters: 550-555 boul. René-Lévesque O Montréal (Québec) H2Z1B1 Canada
India office: 805 Hemkunt House, 8th Floor, Rajendra Place, New Delhi 110008

ISBN: 978-1-4878-0837-2

To find out more about our publications, please visit www.royalcollins.com

Foreword

As the cornerstone of economics, market theory has always dominated its theoretical system with the price mechanism serving as the underlying principle. Separately, it discusses the price mechanism of ordinary goods and Giffen goods in the market. Philosophically, the common mechanism of specific research objects should be characterized by a single rule under uniform theoretical premises. This means that the two-part price mechanism is only an intermediate product in the exploration of market principles.

Nevertheless, economists with gusto still lumped the price mechanism of ordinary goods as a general principle into economic theory. Soon they discovered the price mechanism to be ineffective and in need of refinement. There are many reasons for this: First, the theoretical paradigm of the price mechanism of ordinary goods is premised on perfectly competitive markets.

However, perfectly competitive markets do not exist in reality, but represent a completely abstract, pure state. Second, the theoretical premise of perfectly competitive market has not been upheld in explaining the price mechanism. Instead, perfectly and imperfectly competitive markets coexist as the theoretical premises because only in this way can prices fluctuate. Third, ordinary goods here must face harsh conditions, such as fixed production function, huge market size, rigid demand and supply, and asymmetrical information. Otherwise, price volatility would be impossible. Therefore, they should no longer be called general goods, but only specific agricultural and sideline products, referred to as damping goods in this book. In light of this, economists have patched up market theory with partial corrections. They have introduced concepts such as consumer preference, utility and marginal utility, choice, substitution effect, and income effect – without undermining the underlying price mechanism.

With the development of the economy, the price mechanism fails to explain more and more phenomena. Market equilibrium cannot be achieved, leading to many crises. The production function of almost all industrial products shifts towards cost reduction. In the long-term trend of declining prices of specific industrial products, the supply of such products will first increase and then decrease when the price falls. The demand for some goods tends to expand when the price rises. These goods include financial or quasi-financial products such as houses and stocks, agricultural products such as pork and ginger, and light industrial products such as salt and toilet paper. With the penetration of most durable industrial goods or the emergence of new alternative products, the demand will shrink as the price falls.

This has led to criticism of economic orthodoxy. From the perspective of falsification, if economics is viewed as a science, these cases have been adequately proved wrong. Then, why has this theory been corrected rather than overthrown for so long? It should be noted, that the price mechanism matched people's understanding of economic activities in the early days of great industry because it was a summary of the medieval agricultural market. In the long and slow progress of economic growth, doubts about this theory have been obscured by its revisions.

Such obscuration is uncovered in China's economic development. China's long-term rapid growth embodies the industrialization that Western developed countries had undergone for nearly 300 years. Various economic contradictions have arisen. Pan-Giffen goods that cannot be explained by the price mechanism have appeared frequently in large numbers. Even so, China's regime of mixed economy for market management has achieved greater success than the free market. This fact primarily explains why the falsification of market principles is driven by Chinese scholars.

This book is an English version of some restructured sections of the Chinese version. It would not be published without the support of translator Ms. Joy, lively proofreader Mark, who is also a friend of mine and English teacher, and editors of Royal

Collins Publishing Group. I wish to pay further attention to the theoretical progress of economics and look forward to the establishment of a new theoretical economic system as soon as possible.

Ruyu Zhao
June 2021

Contents

Chapter 1

Market Principles: Exploration and Argument

The advancement of science lies in falsification. Since the inception of economic theories, there have been many doctrines and schools of thought that stick to their own arguments without proving validity. Among them, market principles – as one of the foundations of economics, are both contradictory and controversial. The paradigm of economic theories generally encompass theoretical premises, basic principles, and conclusions. This also applies to market theory. This chapter will examine these paradigm components one by one.

1.1   Betrayal of Prices

The market theory has always been the foundation and theoretical premise of the economic system. The theoretical core consists of general market principles based upon a perfectly competitive market, and explanations for imperfect markets, such as, Giffen goods. However, with the deepening of economic practice, this dual-core market theory is unable to explain new market phenomena in reality. Its flaws have been exposed.

First, market theory holds that in a perfectly competitive market (for ordinary goods): as prices rise, supply increases and demand decreases; as prices fall demand increases and supply decreases.

For Giffen goods of limited supply, such as art objects and stamps: demand increases when prices rise; demand shrinks when prices fall.

However, amid deepening economic activity, many "price failures" cannot be explained by this theory. A large number of goods show the same characteristics as Giffen goods, giving rise to pan-Giffen commercialization. Demand, which increases as prices also rise, occurs with goods subject to moderate or little supply limit, such as stocks, houses, land, salt, washing powder, toilet paper, and other articles for daily use. In the case of economic crisis, demand becomes larger instead of smaller when prices decline. In some under-supplied economies, demand grows regardless of price changes. Therefore, the market theory is not applicable to real market behaviors.

Second, market theory suggests that prices, as market signposts, can effectively regulate market supply and demand, and ultimately balance the allocation of resources towards Pareto optimality. But in fact, the nature of price to betray norms disables the price-based allocation of resources in the market. The economic activities of humans have never reached Pareto efficiency. Without market clearing there are not only frequent economic crises associated with relative over-supply, but also excessive resource waste caused by blind competition. More often than not, market theory is inadequately efficient or even inefficient at guiding economic activities in reality. Such failure indicates the incompetence of market theory.

Third, the above-mentioned theoretical and practical deficiencies reflect the incompleteness of market theory. On the one hand, there is always a basic principle to explain the commonalities of similar things. When two principles are needed to account for one thing or when a principle and its contradictory case coexist, it can be said that these principles do not grasp the basic characteristics of the thing, but give an explanation from one angle or one side by mistaking a part as the whole. Market principles fall into this category. On the other hand, according to the principles of dialectical materialism, there are no absolute truths in the world, but only relative truths that explain recognizable reality for humans. A principle has lost the attribute of relative truth and become a fallacy if any unexplainable phenomena exist. It needs to be updated by a theory and replaced by a new relative truth. In other words, existing market theory cannot fully account for the various phenomena presented by economic activities, and can only discuss superficial characteristics of some market phenomena. In fact, there must be more scientific principles to explain market operation law at a deeper level. It is the purpose of this book to explore and summarize newer and more scientific market principles.

Fourth, market principles ignore transformation of psychological expectation. Market management based on these principles are often counterproductive and lead to worse results. Taking real estate, for example, housing prices rise with the large-scale housing purchase of urban residents. Government authorities take a laissez-faire attitude and even encourage price rises to a sufficient height in the hope of suppressing market demand. Nevertheless, purchases for normal living and investment purposes are profitable, as people have inelastic demand and expect price rises in the long run. As a result, this strategy continues to push up housing prices, creating a huge economic bubble and even jeopardizing national economic security.

In short, due to the nature of prices to betray norms, the price mechanism – which the traditional market theory relies on – fails in resource allocation, leading to overproduction and serious waste of resources. These phenomena underline the absurdity of using price as the "invisible hand" from a realistic perspective.

1.2 Contradictory Theoretical Premises

As mentioned earlier, market theory encompasses principles for ordinary goods and Giffen goods, but the premise varies between these principles. This in itself implies there must be a logical statement that can explain both phenomena under the same premise. Nevertheless, our esteemed economic experts did not challenge the assumption out of respect.

Giffen goods – as an exception to the rule of demand – have been clearly identified as a phenomenon arising in an undersupplied market.[1] Therefore, the focus is put on perfectly competitive markets, defined as a premise for general market theory by the economics community.

A perfectly competitive market is a very well-known hypothesis. It has the following characteristics: i) Players: There are a large number of buyers and sellers without collusion as the effect of an individual can be ignored relative to the entire market; ii) Products: Products are undifferentiated and homogeneous; iii) Barriers: Resources can flow freely; and iv) Information: Information is sufficient and completely symmetrical with slight search costs. The conclusion was summarized by Stigler (1957) based on the studies of Cournot (1838) and Bertrand (1883).[2]

Later, Debreu (1959) presented a behavioral definition of perfect competition based on significant progress in the studies of the Walrasian general equilibrium. Given a series of premises for consumers, businesses, and commodities, utility-maximizing consumers can buy or sell unlimited quantities of commodities at a specific price, and purchases do not affect their profits. In the case when buying or selling any quantity of commodities does not affect price, each business chooses inputs and outputs that maximize net profits. Ultimately, equilibrium is a price vector that represents the choice made by each economic actor, according to prices, to enable market clearing.[3]

Debreu's definition has been recognized globally and is still used today. Deeper studies investigate whether perfect competition can be achieved through imperfect competition. Discussions about imperfect competition theory began as early as the 1930s.

These discussions focused on monopolistic competition, oligopoly, and perfect monopoly. In reality, monopolistic competition is relatively common, while oligopoly and perfect monopoly exist only in a few industries. Chamberlain (1933) made a set of basic assumptions on monopolistic competition, including: i) existence of many firms manufacturing similar products in the market; ii) differences in products of these firms; and iii) no entry or exit barriers for firms. Thus, product differentiation is the distinctive feature and decisive factor of monopolistic competition. Firms make excess profits in the short-run equilibrium under monopolistic competition, which attracts a stream of new firms. As excess profits disappear in the long run, firms obtain normal profits only. Unlike perfect competition, monopolistic competition presents higher price and smaller output at the equilibrium, which implies monopoly waste.[4] Robinson (1933) further divided imperfect competition into monopoly and monopsony, and discussed imperfect competition and the theory of value from the perspectives of factor market and product market.[5] She adopted a different approach from Chamberlain by using marginal analysis. This has evolved into a paradigm for analyzing the theory of the firm in mainstream economics. Based on earlier studies, Dixit (1977) and Stiglitz (1977) proposed the model of imperfect competition involving increasing returns.[6] The Dixit-Stiglitz model is standardized, simple, and easy to use, thus it has been widely applied as a new methodological tool in economic studies.

To sum up, perfect competition is a hypothetical condition favored by research on economic theories, which embodies a research paradigm built from thinking about the law of economic activities in a pure state. In fact, a perfectly competitive market has never happened in reality. The discussions on imperfect competition essentially did not argue against the theoretical premises of market principles. They have unconsciously changed the theoretical premise of perfect competition itself and independently formed a theoretical system. Minor amendments have been subtly made by modern economists – such as recognizing the budget constraints of consumers. However, this is a denial of the premise of infinite demand.

1.3 Traditional Theoretical Logic

The market mechanism operates in a completely different way between ordinary and Giffen goods. In the case of Giffen goods, demand increases and decreases with price. This phenomenon has been recognized as an exception to perfect competition, and has been solidified without undermining the basic premise of perfect competition.

The market mechanism in traditional Western economics is enabled through competition in a perfectly competitive market. It was earliest described by classical economist Adam Smith (1776). The general economic theory integrates this description and suggests that the supply and demand relationship determines the market price of commodities.

Smith believed the market price of commodities can be higher than the natural value where there is a positive difference between the actual demand and supply in the market; otherwise, the market price will be lower than the natural value (Marx, 1894).[7] In a perfectly competitive market, the price of commodities tends to coincide with – and fluctuate around – the natural value. Such competition facilitates a unified profit margin in each economic sector. In the case of undersupply, the competition among consumers will raise the price and increase the profit margin of commodities. Producers will pool capital to these commodities, which alleviates the contradiction between supply and demand. In the case of oversupply, producers will reallocate capital to other commodities. Under this competition mechanism, resources flow freely among various economic sectors until the market price of commodities equal their natural value.[8] This means supply and demand are in equilibrium, and economic activities are balanced.

Marshall (1895) argued the normal value of commodities is related to the cost of production, while market price is mainly influenced by utility and demand.[9] This argument does not affect the core position of Smith's exposition on the market mechanism in economics.

Specifically, according to market principles of classical economics, the price of ordinary goods becomes an "invisible hand" that regulates demand and supply. The market principles for ordinary goods and Giffen goods are as shown in Figure 1–1 and Figure 1–2.

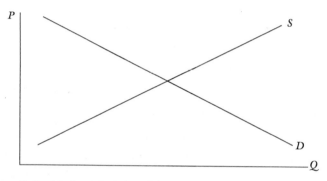

Figure 1–1 Market principles of classical economics for ordinary goods

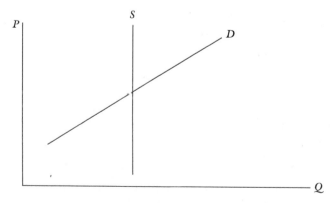

Figure 1–2 Market principles of classical economics for Giffen goods

In brief, in classical economic theory, the market mechanism operates through free competition between supply and demand in a perfectly competitive market. Prices rise or fall as a consequence of supply and demand imbalance, stimulates producers' capital transfer, and further affects the supply and demand relationship. This process is externally manifested in price fluctuations around value.

1.4 Complementary Modern Approach

Based on this, modern economists have fostered a more convincing theoretical paradigm concerning market behavior by integrating such concepts as consumer preference, utility and marginal utility, consumer choice, substitution effect, and income effect. This theoretical paradigm explains, in a wider range of fields, the mechanism of demand changes brought about by supply price fluctuations,[10] as shown in Figure 1–3 and Figure 1–4.

First, consumers are subject to budget constraint. By recognizing this, modern economists effectively denied the traditional assumption that demand is infinite. Second, consumers have different preferences due to various differences. During the buyer decision process, they prioritize preferred goods or bundles, and rationally choose the most useful goods or bundle based on individual differences in the utility of goods. Finally, consumers may choose alternatives due to the impact of changes in their income and commodity prices. The substitution effect

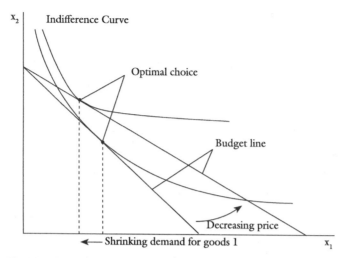

Figure 1-3 Market mechanism of Giffen goods in a modern approach

Source: Varian, H.R. Intermediate Microeconomics: A Modern Approach (Ninth Edition) [M]. New York: W. W. Norton & Company, 2014: 105.

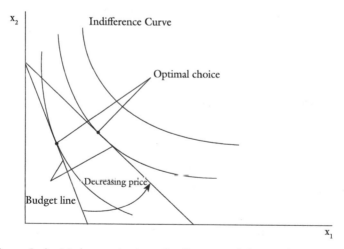

Figure 1-4 Market mechanism of ordinary goods in a modern approach

Source: Varian, H.R. Intermediate Microeconomics: A Modern Approach (Ninth Edition) [M]. New York: W. W. Norton & Company, 2014: 104.

and income effect will further influence consumers' purchasing behavior.

The rise in commodity prices will shift demand to low-cost alternatives within the scope of consumer preferences without changing overall utility; while the decline will lead to a reversed process. Demand may expand by attracting the consumption of alternatives. Income growth will boost the consumption of ordinary goods and reduce the consumption of low-end goods.

The above-mentioned modern approach subtly explains the impact mechanism of price on supply and demand, and incorporates consumer preferences into the analytical framework to illustrate consumer motivation – this complements and improves traditional theories. Nevertheless, these new interpretations examine traditional market principles based on the price mechanism only in the circumstance of relatively sufficient supply and demand, and do not account for the deviation from these principles – such as demand growing or shrinking with prices.

1.5 Reflections on Animals and Gamblers

As economists deepen their understanding of the limitations of market principles, some new explanations have emerged, investigating the market decision-making process through the spiritual world of humans. The incorporation of psychological analysis is undeniably a major advancement in economic theory. However, the exploration has not yet brought about fundamental changes in market principles.

In the late 1970s, behavioral economists analyzed human decision-making processes from a psychological perspective. Kahneman and Tversky (1979) held that the "economic man" assumed in traditional economics has unbounded willpower and pursues utility maximization. In economic practice, however, people tend not to choose the best solution for risk aversion. They take different attitudes toward risks due to differences in the initial situation, and make different choices which are not necessarily rational.[11] Thaler (1980) questioned consumer consciousness in traditional economic assumptions, and argued that consumer choices generally have the endowment effect. In other words, goods that are included in an individual's endowment are more likely to be valued higher (higher than the market value).[12] Further, Thaler (1985) put forward the concept of mental accounting to describe how consumers put more emphasis on mental satisfaction, rather than make rational choices according to the utility-maximizing paradigm.[13]

Rabin (1998) believed that economic practice has proven that traditional economic models are flawed, and that many experimental results called on economists to emphasize psychological and economic integration.[14] Economists such as Hoarth and Kunreuther (1985, 1989, 1990), Camerer (1989), Dekel (1989), Weil (1990), Sarin and Weber (1993), and Machina (1994) have incorporated psychology into their studies. Mullainathan and Thaler (2000) summarized the characteristics of human economic activities as bounded rationality, bounded willpower, and bounded self-interest, further demonstrating the ineffectiveness of the traditional economic paradigm.[15] By establishing a cue-based consumer model, Laibson (2001) provided evidence that consumer perceptions in different contexts have a significant impact on the marginal utility of consumption.[16] Apparently, behavioral economics suggests that given the constraints of environmental uncertainty, incomplete information, and limited cognitive ability, human behavior presents limited rationality rather than complete rationality – with the criteria of satisfactory, rather than optimal choices and decisions, coming into play. This demonstrates the legitimacy of bounded rationality.

George Akerlof and Robert Shiller proposed in their 2009 book *Animal Spirits* that animal spirits determine economic decisions and affect economic operation through five aspects: confidence; fairness; corruption and antisocial behavior; money illusion; and stories.[17]

In this theoretical system, confidence is the cornerstone. It refers to behavior that cannot be covered by rational decision-making. At the macroeconomic level, confidence is sometimes reasonable and sometimes unreasonable. It is more than rational prediction, but also the most important factor in animal spirits. Confidence also has a multiplier effect. To this end, the government's crisis policy should pay attention to credit crunches associated with low confidence and further manage the credit flow above the level of full-employment.

The attitude towards fairness largely determines the setting of wages and prices. People feel happy mainly because the expected targets are achieved. In this sense, people expect fairness, which is a major motivation for economic decision-making. Related to confidence, fairness can easily explain the relationships between involuntary unemployment, inflation, and gross product as well as similar economic phenomena.

The temptation towards corruption and antisocial behavior is undeniable. Economic fluctuations are partly attributed to changing levels and acceptance of corruption during different periods, and more importantly, to shifts that antisocial behavior permeates (that is, economic activity, while technically legal, has sinister motives). John Galbraith pointed out that antisocial behavior increased (the misappropriation of public funds increased rapidly) during economic expansion and was discovered after economic collapse. Every recession is accompanied by corruption and fraud.

Money illusion is the second cornerstone of this theory. The public is tempted by the nominal value of money, and confused about inflation or deflation and even their effects. Wage contracts, price decisions, bond contracts, and account books fail to weaken the effects of inflation through index adjustment. If the money illusion is accounted for, completely different policy conclusions will be drawn in macroeconomics.

Inspiring stories provide an object of reference for public action. People are motivated in various ways after experiencing these types of stories. They also account for the confidence of a country, a firm, or an institution. Confidence is often boosted by inspiring stories that are related to the development of new business and the magical accumulation of wealth.

Theoretical exploration stops with many questions left unsolved. It is found that confidence results from certain trends in economic activity. When the economic situation improves, confidence rises and promotes economic prosperity; and conversely, when an economy declines, confidence weakens and further leads to severe economic depression. This means that confidence is a product of economic activity, rather than a decisive factor. In addition, fairness as an important principle of market exchange, is an essential factor. However, the theory fails to explain the criteria and determiner of fairness. Obviously, the fairness of exchange is determined by the demand side, and the individual's grasp of fairness is determined by bounded rationality based on available information. Similarly, corruption and antisocial behavior are the companions to crisis and prosperity. Money illusion does not affect the existence and change of the economic cycle.

So, what is the "invisible hand" that really decides market behavior?

Endnotes

1. In the 19th century, Robert Giffen found that the potato demand increased as the price rose. Later, commodities with such phenomena, such as art objects and stamps, are called Giffen goods. In this regard, David Ricardo said that commodities derive their exchangeable value from two sources: from their scarcity, and from the quantity of labor required to obtain them. There are some commodities with the value entirely governed by their scarcity alone, such as, pictures, scarce books, and coins (Ricardo, D. On the Principle of Political Economy and Taxation. In The Works and Correspondence of David Ricardo, Vol. I. ed. P. Sraffa, Cambridge University Press, 1951: 12). In 1895, Marshall first incorporated the concept of "Giffen goods"

in economics textbooks. Marshall, A. Principles of Economics [M]. Cambridgeshire: Cambridge University Press, 1895: 78–96.

2. Stigler, G. Perfect Competition, Historically Contemplated [J]. Journal of Political Economy. 1957 (65): 1–17; Cournot, A. Recherchssur Les Princips the Mathèmatiques de La Thèorie des Richesses [M] Paris: M. Rivière, 1838. Bertrand, J. Thèorie Mathèmatique de La Richesse Cociale [J]. Journal des Savante. 1883 (48): 499–508.

3. Debreu, G. The Theory of Value [M]. New York: Joun Wiley & Sons, 1959. Quoted from the New Palgrave Dictionary of Economics [M]. Beijing: Economics Science Press, 1996: 897.

4. Chamberlin E. H. The Theory of Monopolistic Competition [M]. Cambridge: Harvard University Press, 1956.

5. Robinson. The Economics of Imperfect Competition [M]. Basingstoke: Palgrave MacMillan, 1969.

6. Dixit A. K, Stiglitz J.S. Monopolistic Competition and Optimum Product Diversity [J]. American Economic Review, 1977 (3): 297–308.

7. In this regard, Marx (Marx, 1894) pointed out in *Capital* that the so-called natural value of goods should be determined by the socially necessary labor time.

8. Smith A. An Inquiry into the Nature and Causes of the Wealth of Nations [M]. Oxford: Oxford University, 1776: 73–74.

9. Marshall A. Principles of Economics [M]. Cambridgeshire: Cambridge University Press, 1895.

10. Varian, H.R. Intermediate Microeconomics: A Modern Approach (Ninth Edition) [M]. W. W. Norton & Company, New York, 2010: 88.

11. Kahneman D., Tversky A. Prospect Theory: An Analysis of Decision under Risk [J]. Econometrica, 1999, 47 (2): 263–292.

12. Thaler R. Toward a Positive Theory of Consumer Choices [J]. Journal of Economic Behavior and Organization, 1980, 1 (1): 39–60.

13. Thaler R. Mental Accounting and Consumer Choice [J]. Marketing Science, 1985, 4 (3): 199–214.

14. Rabin M. Psychology and Economics [J]. Journal of Economic Literature, 1998, 36 (1): 11–46.

15. Mullainathan S, Thaler R. Behavioral Economics [Z]. NBER Working Paper No. 7948, Oct. 2000.

16. Laibson D. A Cue–Theory of Consumption [J]. The Quarterly Journal of Economics, 2001, 116 (1): 81–119.

17. Akerlof G.A, Shiller R. J. Animal Spirits: How Human Psychology Drives the Economy and Why It Matters for Global Capitalism [M]. New York: Princeton University Press, 2009.

Chapter 2

Reflections on Smith: Limitations of the Times

As mentioned earlier, market principles that take the price mechanism as the theoretical lynchpin often fail to guide real economic activities due to low efficiency or inefficiency.

2.1   Adam Smith's Market Principles

The price mechanism is the theoretical core of market principles. Classical economist Adam Smith (*Wealth of Nations*, 1776) is the first to describe the price mechanism. Upholding his philosophy, the general economic theory considers the supply and demand relationship as the determiner of market price of goods.

Specifically, when supply falls far short of actual demand, the price will rise to far exceed the natural value (i.e., production cost), which Marx pointed out should be determined by socially necessary labor time. In a perfectly competitive market, this situation will stimulate the flow of social capital, labor, and other resources to the line of production of these goods. As production expansion alleviates the shortage of supply, the market price will decline, leaving smaller room for production profits. The inflows of capital and labor will diminish and even become outflows to areas with higher profits. Contrarily, an excess supply will drive the price down to far below the natural value (i.e., production cost). In a perfectly competitive market, social capital, labor, and other resources will withdraw from the line of production.

Smith held that free competition in a perfectly competitive market will enable the market price of commodities to fluctuate around the natural value (Figure 2–1). Resources flow without barriers among various economic sectors until the market price equals the natural value.[1] In this case, supply and demand are

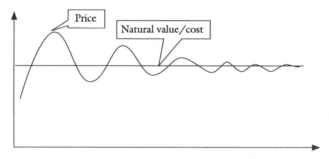

Figure 2–1   Price mechanism of ordinary goods in Adam Smith's theory

in equilibrium, and each economic sector has formed a unified profit margin in the chain of economic activities. Equilibrium herein is a state in which production is equal to consumption and price is equal to cost.

The definition from Debreu (1959) further highlighted perfect competition as the premise of the price mechanism. According to his definition (refer to page 6 herein), fully rational consumers (utility-maximizing) and suppliers (return-maximizing) face infinite supply and infinite demand (commodities can be bought or sold in unlimited quantities at a specific price) and achieve equilibrium under the conditions of perfect competition (market clearing can be achieved). This definition-based description implies that competition in a perfectively competitive market is 'perfect competition.' It precisely serves to endorse Adam Smith's theory that market clearing can be achieved in a perfectly competitive market.

2.2 Logical Flaws of the Price Mechanism

The fatal flaws of the theoretical paradigm are fundamentally responsible for the increasing inadequacies of the price mechanism in interpreting and guiding reality. These flaws include the obvious contradiction between the premise and conclusion, the particularity of the price fluctuation mechanism, and the falsity of treating special cases as general ones.

2.2.1 Contradiction between Premise and Conclusion

The theoretical premise of the price mechanism is perfect competition, and the conclusion is market clearing achieved through price-based allocation of resources. However, there is an inherent contradiction.

In terms of premise, in a perfectly competitive market, supply and demand are sufficient, and information is completely symmetrical. It means that producers know how much consumers need and consumers know how much producers provide. In this case, how does the gap between supply and demand arise? To take a step back, even if there is an initial difference, supply is sufficient and unlimited, as it is can enter the market without cost at any time to instantly compensate for the shortage. Similarly, full and unlimited demand can enter the market without cost at any time to meet the surplus of supply. Then, how does the price differ from the natural value? Since the initial difference between supply and demand and the price departure from natural value are not the same, then how does price repeatedly fluctuate around the natural value? The conclusion that prices fluctuate around the natural value and finally reach market equilibrium is logically untenable.

Thus, the price mechanism essentially accounts for the market phenomena of "ordinary goods" in a real imperfectly competitive market – its assumption of perfectly competitive markets does not exist in reality.

2.2.2 Particularity of "Ordinary Goods"

In the price volatility mechanism described by Smith, "ordinary goods" are not representative of the real world, but only limited to a handful of specific commodities.

According to realistic conditions for the price mechanism, "ordinary goods" should have the following attributes: i) Relatively stable natural value – the production function remains basically the same in more than one supply/demand cycle. Only in this way can price fluctuations be targeted; ii) Huge market capacity. The difference between supply and demand is enough to cause huge price changes; iii) Relatively rigid demand. Demand cannot be expanded accordingly to cover the excess supply. Where supply falls short, alternatives may be selected to meet demand while adequately increasing supply. In other words, demand shrinks/expands to a limited extent when the price rises/declines; iv) Moderately rigid supply. The surplus of supply cannot be stored until the next demand cycle and is left only to the market. The shortage of supply cannot be replenished, which means new supply is not available in a demand cycle due to long production cycle; v) Serious information asymmetry of supply and demand. This is especially true when suppliers find difficulty in obtaining information from each other, posing huge uncertainty in the production process, or when they are relatively isolated from information; and vi) The supply and demand sides need multiple cycles to gradually acquire sufficient information for prices and natural values to be generally consistent.

Given the said conditions, it can be found that so-called "ordinary goods" are not ordinary commodities, but specific commodities, such as agricultural and sideline products including grain, fruit, pork, beef, and mutton. Their production function is relatively stable over the long term, and market capacity for supply and demand is extremely large. The demand is rigid as there are both upper and lower limits for basic physiological needs, such as grain. The supply cannot be added in a timely manner to meet the demand due to long production cycle. Grain production requires at least a few months or even one year, and pig production requires nearly one year. Moreover, grain production suffers weather-related uncertainty and supply information asymmetry between regions. Most of the surplus products cannot be stored until the next cycle. Stocked grain and frozen pork will find no space as newly yielded grain and pigs occupy the market in the second year. Therefore, the surplus supply will be sold at a price lower than the production cost – price equals cost in Adam Smith's equilibrium, which is to some extent attributed to people's rational pursuit of profit maximization or loss minimization. In reality, farmers may suffer when grain becomes cheap following a bumper harvest, and consumers may tolerate a price rise in the rush to purchase goods in short supply out of basic physiological considerations.

To sum up, the "ordinary goods" in Adam Smith's theory are by no means ordinary. They are agricultural commodities with long production cycles and large supply uncertainty as well as other commodities with similar characteristics, which should not simply be deemed agricultural and sideline products.

Herein, such commodities are referred to as "damping goods"[2] to facilitate further analysis of inherent deficiencies in Adam Smith's theory of price mechanism.

2.2.3. Limitations of Damping Goods

Ordinary goods in Adam Smith's theory are damping goods with specific attributes, mainly comprised of agricultural products. With a price volatility mechanism different from general industrial products and pan-Giffen goods, damping goods are not representative of ordinary goods.

General industrial products act completely differently from damping goods. First, the production function is in a constant state of flux because the value of general industrial products is not fixed. Generally, the price shows a downward trend – mostly due to the decline in cost. There are various factors at play, including innovation in production processes, raw materials and sales channels, productivity growth by division of labor and proficiency, labor cost decline (labor saving or automation), and reduction of costs brought by economies of scale. Second, the demand for general industrial products is not relatively rigid – it does not fall into the minimum physiological needs of humans, and it gradually rises as income increases. Therefore, when the price drops in the case of excess supply, the demand can be expanded or even fully satisfied. When the price rises in the case of inadequate supply, alternatives can be selected or given up if similar goods are unaffordable. Third, the supply of general industrial products has strong price elasticity. The surplus of supply can be stored for the next demand cycle, and production can be halted at any time for withdrawal from the market. The shortage of supply can be alleviated by additional supply as producers can expand production capacity in a timely manner. Fourth, despite information asymmetry between suppliers and consumers, it is relatively easy for suppliers to exchange information, which prevents huge uncertainty in the production process. Fifth, when an industrial product in its lifecycle is replaced with the evolution of consumption structure, its price will gradually decline to below its cost. At this time, the product will basically withdraw from the market permanently. This does not happen to bulk agricultural products, such as grain, where price decline is limited to a single cycle. Sixth, in a perfectly competitive market, equilibrium can be theoretically reached for general industrial products. In practice, however, imbalance is normal in a real imperfectly competitive market – manifested in many historical economic crises of overproduction. The price volatility of general industrial products is shown in Figure 2–2.

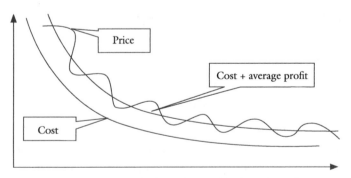

Figure 2–2 Price volatility of general industrial products

Evidently, the market price of agricultural products revolves around the natural value. Unlike this, the market price of general industrial products fluctuates around the manufacturing price under the premise of maximizing profit. Since the manufacturing price equals the sum of cost and average profit, the fluctuating price usually stays above the cost. In individual cases, the market price of specific industrial products to be replaced and delisted may be lower than the production cost. It is a market strategy of manufacturers to maximize profits or minimize losses based on marginal thinking when they have basically achieved the profit target.

It is not difficult to observe Adam Smith's concept of price mechanism took only the price volatility of agricultural products into account because he lived during the early stages of the British industrial revolution. The included cases (damping goods) cannot represent general industrial products dominant in industrial society since they fail to account for the market mechanism of industrial society. This is the historical limitation of Smith's theory of market principles and price mechanism.

2.3 Philosophical Incompleteness of Market Principles

In addition to huge logical flaws and historical limitations of the price mechanism, Adam Smith's entire theoretical system of market principles is philosophically incomplete. It is manifested in two aspects: i) With dual theoretical paradigms – there are no unified theoretical premises, theoretical core, or conclusions; and ii) Even in the same theoretical paradigm, the theoretical premises are inconsistent and chaotic.

2.3.1 Dual-core Framework of Theoretical Paradigm

As discussed earlier, Adam Smith's market principles consist of two components: the price volatility mechanism of "ordinary goods" premised on perfectly competitive markets and the explanation on price changes of Giffen goods in limited supply premised on imperfectly competitive markets. Among them, "ordinary goods" have been discussed in detail in the preceding sections. Giffen goods refer to commodities for which the demand increases as the price rises. The concept was proposed by British scholar Robert Giffen in the 19th century after finding that the demand for potatoes increased as the price rose. Later, the term was used to refer to commodities with similar features, such as art objects, stamps, and ancient coins. In modern economic activities, Giffen goods are generalized as stocks, houses, some agricultural products, and even industrial products such as toilet paper and salt.

It is not difficult to find that two theoretical paradigms coexist in Smith's market principles, based on the following evidence: i) Two theoretical premises: the perfectly competitive market of "ordinary goods" and imperfectly competitive market of Giffen goods; ii) Two price change mechanisms. For "ordinary goods," the demand shrinks and the supply increases when the price goes up, and the demand expands and the supply decreases when the price goes down. For Giffen goods, the demand grows as the price rises and diminishes as the price falls; and iii) Two results of market operations. Market equilibrium can be achieved for "ordinary goods" through price fluctuations around natural values, but it is impossible for Giffen goods.

From a philosophical standpoint, the development of everything has its own inherent regularity which can be scientifically summarized by employing a basic theoretical paradigm. However, traditional market principles prevail with two concurrent theoretical paradigms. This philosophical incompleteness is concealed in the deceptive general law – Smith took damping goods as representative of only a few commodities (as ordinary goods) of universal significance; however, as aforementioned, the "ordinary goods" referred to by Smith are just damping goods that form a small portion of commodities with specific properties. Smith's summary of market rules is limited to damping goods and Giffen goods, two special commodity groups. It does not cover all market phenomena or represent all commodity groups. Thus, Adam Smith's market principles have yet to find an element basic enough to explain all market phenomena or a unified theoretical premise.

2.3.2 Chaos of the Theoretical Premise

Even in the theoretical paradigm for "ordinary goods," the premises are contradictory. A perfectly competitive market is a precondition in Smith's analysis. However, the departure of price from the natural value was first proposed in the specific analysis of the price volatility process. This departure is simply impossible in a perfectly competitive market, and oversupply or undersupply can only occur under the conditions of imperfect competition. Here, Smith unemotionally integrated imperfect competition as a premise in its analytical framework. According to his logic, facing the imbalance between supply and demand caused by imperfect competition, both supply and demand sides adjust the allocation of social resources by price under the premise of perfect competition – yet, due to imperfect competition, the problem cannot be solved immediately and must rely on price volatility resulting from the automatic adjustment of supply and demand in a perfectly competitive market.

In terms of the conclusions of market principles for "ordinary goods," the market balance achieved through the price mechanism: supply = demand, price = cost, and market clearing only exists in a perfectly competitive market. This is because price will never equal cost, even though supply sometimes equals demand in reality. It is in the agrarian society – before the industrialization – that price covers cost only. For example, the price of agricultural products, production tools, and daily necessities produced by handicrafts can simply be regarded as basic raw materials plus labor compensation. Moreover, the land rent included in the price of agricultural products must also be regarded as land costs, with the exploitation herein ignored. However, this situation only applies to agrarian society. In industrial societies, the capitalist mode of production occupies a dominant position. Industrial products that account for the vast majority of the market are no longer cleared by cost only, but by cost plus return on capital (that is residual value). Therefore, the conclusions Adam Smith drew from his market principles also depart from reality and only account for perfectly competitive markets in agrarian societies.

Imperfectly competitive and perfectly competitive markets are used inconsistently – both independently and in combination, by traditional economic theories and the price mechanism for "ordinary goods." The philosophical incompleteness inevitably undermines the scientific nature of the conclusions. In fact, the price mechanism of Adam Smith's market theory only reflects local markets during specific time periods, rather than the whole market system. Market clearing has never appeared. More often than not, economists are forced to investigate the problem of market failure.

2.4 Market Principles under Perfect Competition

As mentioned earlier, Smith's classic economic theory is philosophically incomplete in nature. It allowed for the exception of Giffen goods in perfectively competitive markets and recognized two kinds of premises and market mechanisms. The market principles for ordinary goods also have many theoretical loopholes: i) The concepts of Perfect market and Imperfect market are confused in the premises; ii) If a market is completely competitive, there will be no price volatility or price mechanism for adjusting resource allocation; and iii) "Ordinary goods" are not universal at all. They can only represent a certain portion of bulk agricultural products ("damping goods"). Therefore, the market described by Smith is not Perfect in the true sense. Thus, market principles cannot fully explain the fluctuation of supply and demand, whether in a perfectly competitive market or not.

To this end, this author tries to re-summarize the fluctuation mechanism of commodity supply and demand under the conditions of perfect competition.

2.4.1 Perfectly Competitive Market and a Pure Economy

First, with respect for the summarizations made by academics (Debreu, 1959), a perfectly competitive market is usually defined to have the following characteristics: i) unlimited supply and demand; ii) no entry or exit barriers (in space, time, technology, and finance); iii) completely symmetrical information (sufficient information with no cost); and iv) perfectly rational economic agents pursuing optimal outcomes in both supply and demand.

There are two ways for information exchange to support perfect information symmetry. The first is to use market price as the medium. The departure of market price from the natural value of commodity (i.e., the cost of commodity)[3] can be transmitted to all consumers and suppliers in an immediate, unobstructed, and complete manner. Under this price-based information transmission mechanism, the difference in market price implies the difference in quantity between supply and demand. This leads us to summarize market principles based on the price mechanism. The second way is to use the social network as the medium. In the social network of a pure economy, the quantity of goods needed exactly matches the quantity of goods provided. Compared with price, social networks offer a more direct way of transmitting supply and demand information in line with the characteristics of a pure economy; there is a perfectly symmetrical transmission mechanism for price information.

2.4.2 Price Mechanism under the Premise of a Perfectly Competitive Market

In a perfectly competitive market with unlimited supply and demand, and when information is symmetrically transmitted via price, market equilibrium can be achieved immediately by adjusting market supply and demand.

As shown in Figure 2–3, when the price P_1 is higher than the natural value of commodity P_2, it means supply falls short of demand. In this case, since economic activities are aimed at satisfying demand and supply can be expanded indefinitely, the pathway to market equilibrium is very simple – instantly expanding supply to the quantity required by demand, thus achieving and maintaining market equilibrium. The instant

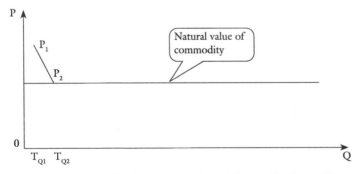

Figure 2–3 Relationship between supply and demand in the perfectly competitive market with price as the medium (Initially, supply is less than demand)

expansion of supply means that the time for transition from Q_1 to Q_2 is as close as possible to zero, that is, $\Delta T \to 0$ ($\Delta T = T_{Q2} - T_{Q1}$).

As shown in Figure 2–4, when the price is lower than the natural commodity value, it means supply exceeds demand. In this case, demand can be expanded or supply reduced. However, it should be noted that demand is not subject to quantity or cost limitation, and market demand should fully reflect all needs. It is illogical to expand demand for the purpose of market equilibrium. Since there is no quantity limit on supply and cost for market entry and exit, supply should be instantly withdrawn from the market to make commodity prices completely equal to natural values, so that market equilibrium can be realized and maintained. Similarly, the instant reduction of supply means that the time for transition from Q_1 to Q_2 is as close as possible to zero, that is, $\Delta T \to 0$ ($\Delta T = T_{Q2} - T_{Q1}$).

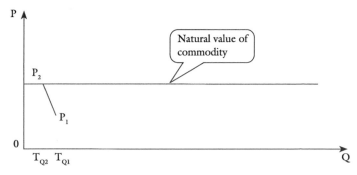

Figure 2–4 Relationship between supply and demand in the perfectly competitive market with price as the medium (Initially, supply is more than demand)

2.4.3 Social Network Mechanism under the Premise of Perfectly Competitive Market

In a perfectly competitive market, information transmission through social network covers transmission before production and at the time of market entry and thereafter. Such information transmission has sufficient symmetry; otherwise, price information will not be fully symmetrical. The contributive social network can fully share supply and demand information before the commodity enters the market, and the supply and demand relationship determines the price to facilitate full information symmetry of the pure economy.

Then, how are supply and demand adjusted in perfectly competitive markets? Given information symmetry and the information transmission mechanism via social network, market equilibrium will be naturally achieved at the end of production process (before entering the market) – commodities are produced

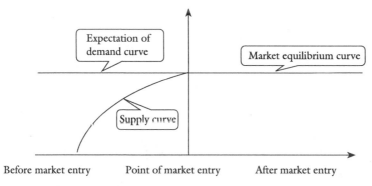

Figure 2–5　Relationship between supply and demand in the perfectly competitive market with social network as the medium

in accordance with quantity expectation, thus there is no difference in price and quantity between supply and demand. The market is in equilibrium after the commodity enters the market, as shown in Figure 2–5.

2.4.4 Summary of Market Mechanism in the Perfectly Competitive Market

Under the premise of perfect competition, market resource allocation through multiple price fluctuations is impossible due to infinite, immediate, and unobstructed supply and full information symmetry. All differences in the quantity between supply and demand can be immediately eliminated by the scaling down or up of supply. Therefore, where information is transmitted by means of price, the market mechanism premised on perfect competition is a one-off adjustment and restoration of continuous market equilibrium. Where information is transmitted through the social network, market equilibrium has been realized as early as commodity production, therefore, the entire market is in a state of natural equilibrium. Thus, social network is more suitable for the pure economy.

It should be emphasized that demand is inelastic, thus largely irrelevant in adjusting the supply and demand relationship. Demand is the fundamental driving force of human economic activities; it is demand that makes supply necessary. Supply is sufficient, unlimited, immediate, and free to enter and exit the market. Therefore, the relationship between market supply and demand can be adjusted by changing supply rather than demand. Under the price mechanism, when the price is too low, it is impossible to stimulate demand due to its inelasticity in a perfectly competitive market. In this case, supply should be reduced to adapt to fully manifested demand. When the price is too high, it is not suitable to reduce demand to balance the market. The passive reduction of demand means the market has failed to fully satisfy demand. This runs away from the original intention of market activities. Therefore, the appropriate solution for perfectly competitive markets should be to immediately expand supply to satisfy demand.

In short, under the premise of perfect competition, market demand does not need adjustment, and market supply can be expanded or reduced according to the requirements of demand. Where information is transmitted by means of price, supply should be adjusted to conform to demand, so that the price of a commodity equals its natural value. The adjustment is an immediate process with a one-off price movement. Where social network serves as the medium for information transmission, supply has been aligned in quantity with demand before entering the market. The market naturally reaches the equilibrium state without even moving.

Endnotes

1. Smith A. An Inquiry into the Nature and Causes of the Wealth of Nations [M]. Oxford: Oxford University, 1776, 73–78.

2. In physics, damping refers to the characteristic that the amplitude of vibration in any vibration system gradually decays due to external influences

or inherent system cause. Drawing on this concept, "damping goods" are used to define specific commodities proposed in Adam Smith's theory of price mechanism, whose price volatility amplitude decreases in the long run to bring prices in conformity to the natural values.

3. The price is compared with the natural value because the assumed pure state of economy does not include any factors of imperfectly competitive market, such as profit and excess profit.

Chapter 3

The imperfect market: Era of the Wise Man

As stated earlier, traditional market theory is fundamentally flawed, where the theoretical premise of ordinary goods seriously deviates from reality. Since the perfectly competitive market underpinning market theory is detached from economic reality, the market mechanism will also be flawed. In light of this, modern Western economists proposed the substitution and income effects to interpret the relationship between supply and demand. They tended to describe the specific performance of the market in real economic activities, which intentionally obscured, rather than explicitly denied, a perfectly competitive market as the premise of classical theory. Apparently, Western economics follows the theoretical tradition of classical economics, and places hope on reality to offset and resolve the flawed theoretical premise. The human practice of economic activities has proved that there is no perfect competition in the market. Price has never, as the "invisible hand," enabled the optimal allocation of social and economic resources or market clearing.

To this end, the book reexamines and explores the principles of market behavior by starting from reality. Based on the understanding of market imperfection, the theoretical premise of market principles is set in an imperfect market.

3.1 Reset of the Premises

An imperfect market has the following characteristics: i) There is no infinite supply or infinite demand in economic activities; ii) Consumers and producers are subject to various obstacles to market entry, such as space, policy, technology, and cost; iii) Products are differentiated and qualitatively heterogeneous, though substitutable; iv) Information is insufficient and generally asymmetric, mainly due to information search costs. In addition, consumers are irrational, unlike the premise of classical theory that there are neither omniscient gods[1] nor irrational actors.[2] For this reason, the era of market economy is herein referred to as the era of the Wise Man – an era paradoxically dominated by intelligent humans and constrained by human intelligence.

It should be noted that the definition of an imperfect market is much broader than the "imperfectly competitive market" – the latter being merely a result of monopoly. An imperfect market comprises of monopoly, as well as limitations of supply and demand, spatial heterogeneity, individual heterogeneity (including labor heterogeneity), asymmetric information, etc. In this sense, we deliberately use the denotation of "imperfect market" as be distinct from "imperfectly competitive market."

This definition of imperfect market faithfully describes the reality of economic activities. Since inception, human economic activities have been restricted by resource limitation and spatial heterogeneity, and are unable to support supply and demand without limits. The traditional market theory lacks explanatory power because it assumed a perfectively competitive market that does not exist. Classical economists who proposed this theory ignored resource limitation, space existence, and heterogeneity in the name of academia – in order to serve market expansion needs of capitalist interests in the United Kingdom at the time.

It should be noted that Adam Smith's market principles also deliberately ignored market imperfection to make up for limitations in the endorsement of the bourgeoisie. Adam Smith and David Ricardo suggested countries make use of their absolute or comparative advantages in the international division of labor, implying the division of labor can be infinitely extended without minding the quantity difference between demand and supply. In fact, Britain mainly exported industrial products like textiles at the time, for which demand could grow with income and supply could be expanded more by increasing global resources. Other countries mainly held advantage in agricultural products. In the case of French wine in the classical theory, the demand is subject to customer preferences and affordability, and the supply is restricted by spatial heterogeneity. Clearly, the advent and promotion of this theory drove industrialization in the interest of the British bourgeoisie.

In reality, only a cruel imperfect market exists, based on the following observations:

(1) Economic resources are limited. The Earth we live in has vast land and rich resources, but the available space and economic resources are ultimately limited. Coupled with technological limitations, it is impossible for humans to use all the resources on Earth or to use every resource absolutely. Economics thus emerged to address the choice of limited and scarce resources for the production of goods to meet current and future social needs. On this fundamental proposition of economics to be dealt with, economists have already formed a consensus based on full understanding. Therefore, the assumption of infinite supply in the premise of a perfectively competitive market is not correct, whether in terms of quantity or variety of products.

The Earth's resources are limited not only in absolute quantity, but also relative to the population, lifestyle, and technological means of humans. As known to all, the human population is growing year by year, with 4.3 newborns per second and an annual addition of about 82.96 million. The number will approximately climb from the current 7.4 billion to 9 billion in 2050. While poor industrial technologies and rising living standards are rapidly draining the Earth of resources, pollutants emitted by humans are eroding their living space. In view of this, almost everyone will no longer believe that supply is infinite.

From the perspective of demand, although desire is unlimited, paying ability is ultimately limited; this condition is restricted by the production of labor forces and physical products.

(2) Space exists objectively and has heterogeneity, which has a decisive influence on market imperfection. Firstly, as objective and rational economic actors, humans can only depend on specific geographical space, in which supply is further restricted by limited resources. Secondly, climate, geography, and such elements of specific geographical space determine the earliest industrial formation and development. Animal husbandry, hunting, and fishing industries develop in steppes, forests and lakes, while farming took shape in plain areas with water access and vegetation. The industrial difference resulting from spatial heterogeneity not only further limits the quantity and variety of supply, but also fundamentally determines the limited quantity and variety of demand. Thirdly, space objectively creates barriers to entry for consumers, suppliers, means of production, and information. Spatial intervention increases the cost of market entry through distance and terrain changes such as mountains and rivers. Moreover, spatial heterogeneity leads to the natural segmentation of the market, which adds information search cost and causes the natural asymmetry of market information. In addition, spatial isolation allows for

different production experiences and consumption habits of people, giving rise to different social civilizations. Cultural heterogeneity allows for different perceptions of economic activities. As a result, production information becomes asymmetric and misplaced.

Regional heterogeneity and spatial constraint evidently manifest in our daily lives. Taking French wine as an example, grape growing is subject to such restraints as climate and soil. It is impossible for Eskimos to plant grapes in extremely hot equatorial regions, let alone on the ice sheets. Economic products originally produced in a region usually form a tradition that significantly distinguishes this region from others. For example, China's Loess Plateau is known for millet. Although there are some other areas on the planet with similar latitude and soil condition, this type of nutritious millet is not knowingly produced in North America or northern Europe. Spatial distance and associated cultural discrepancy undoubtedly hinder the acquisition of market information, which makes it possible for heterogeneous cultures to raise the price or commit market fraud.

(3) Both consumers and producers are bounded rational people. In the pursuit of maximum interests, they as individuals can only rely on information obtained by themselves in the decision-making process of economic activities. Their understanding of the law of economic activities is constrained by various factors, including incomplete and asymmetrical information, heterogeneity of production and

consumption habits and social culture, and limited cognitive capability of natural world and social phenomena. Hence, the maximization of interests pursued by market players is limited to an individual's own understanding.

Humans are far from being omniscient. The choice of economic resources and production techniques is limited by cognitive ability. For example, during the first industrial revolution, steam engines designed by James Watt helped London rid its dependence on water. With the advent of steam engines, forests were devastated in Britain because people chose charcoal to heat the water used in steam engines. After charcoal was banned, people turned their eyes to coal, which has limited supply.

Besides, human perception of economic activities is also bounded. For instance, people blindly believe that the rise in prices can curb demand, so they give free reign to housing prices in the hope of demand decline at an upcoming turning point towards market balance and a peaceful world. As a result, however, housing prices surge endlessly, and plunge when beyond the support of financial liquidity, leading to the collapse of the entire economy. The collapse of the Japanese bubble economy in the 1990s and the American financial crisis of 2008/09 are examples of this.

The bounded rationality of people is reflected in the inadequate understanding of society and nature. Due to such inadequacy, the decision-making in economic activities is always rationally bounded. In reality, people do not have unlimited willpower or necessarily pursue utility maximization. Restricted by information acquisition, people often choose acceptable suboptimal products for the sake of lower information costs – such as time and money spent on comparing the price and performance of products in different places. They prefer to choose a relatively safe combination of commodities to avoid risks and secure suboptimal returns, rather than risk losing all returns or even paying sunk costs for optimal returns. Such practice is more prominent in areas like gambling.

People as emotional animals tend to unconsciously consider goods in their possession more valuable because such goods usually embody their life processes. As a result of mental accounting, consumers make bounded rational choices based on commodity demand, psychological demand, and perception of limited supply, rather than the so-called rational choice that follows the utility maximization paradigm of economics.

In recent years, in-depth studies have been conducted on the influence of psychological factors on consumer rationality. Some scholars suggested that people show bounded rationality, willpower, and self-interest in economic activities. Behavioral economists generally believed people have bounded behavioral rationality and usually make suboptimal choices that can basically satisfy their needs. This choice model is precisely and objectively attributed to imperfect competition. Spatial obstacles prevent people from understanding the whole picture and avoiding spatial costs such as distance, terrain and climate. Temporal obstacles are likely to cause time lags in understanding and decision-making. Inadequate understanding of nature and society very often restrict the choice of market techniques and commodity functions. Obstacles to market competition, such as real market monopoly, policy-based market segmentation, and national protectionism, indirectly affect consumer choice of commodity prices by limiting the scope of commodity circulation. Ultimately, all these factors lead to bounded rationality.

In short, imperfect market exists in reality. The pure state deliberately abstracted against this reality is no help to develop a theory consistent with market reality.

3.2 Simple Market Principle

In imperfect competition, demand, rather than supply, ultimately decides trading behavior, in which expectations really serve as the "invisible hand." The expectations of demand emerge earlier and play a dominant role in market behavior, while the expectations of supply lags behind and play a subordinate role. The basic mechanism of impact on demand is described as follows: As consumer expectations grow, demand expands and drives up supply by raising supplier expectations; and as consumer expectations decline, demand shrinks and drives down supply by lowering supplier expectations. It is precisely because of the objective existence of imperfect competition that market imbalance is inevitable and market management is necessary. At present, social and economic development has reached the stage of supply management. On the one hand, market management should shift from low-level, supply-oriented demand management to advanced, scientific, and demand-oriented supply management, and from overall and approximate to strict and targeted supply management. With the support of modern information technology such as big data and cloud computing, supply will be directed towards on-demand production, and gradually accumulate and pave the material foundation for on-demand distribution. On the other hand, in order to meet the group needs for environmental protection and resource sustainability, supply management should consciously guide eco-friendly social supply for the purpose of sustainable development for all.

Endnotes

1. Rational people in classical economics actually, like gods, have enough economic knowledge to understand everything in economic activities.

2. In *Animal Spirits* authored by George Akerlof and Robert Schiller, the bounded human rationality in economic activities is coarsely described as animal instinct, including confidence, fairness, corruption and antisocial behavior, money illusion, and stories. This description obviously denotes superficial intuition without in-depth analysis. Please refer to Chapter 1 for relevant discussions.

Chapter 4

The Market Determiner: Expectations

The market is indisputably an essential element of economic activity. The Earth we live on exists and operates in its own way – no matter whether you know that the Earth is a planet in the solar system that rotates on its axis and revolves around the Sun. The Sun still rises in the East and sets in the West, even if you are certain that the Sun revolves around the Earth without paying attention to other stars. Just like the Earth, the market operates in its own way, though price is not really the decisive power.

4.1 Source Analysis: Market Formation

The market forms after human activities of understanding and transforming nature reach a certain stage. In general, the exchangeable surplus of material products to requirements for daily life is essential for the emergence of economically meaningful markets. More importantly, the need for exchange is crucial to market formation for four reasons.

(1) The surplus of products only offers a possibility for conversion into supply and function as a medium of payment for exchange. In other words, the surplus solves the problem of supply and payment capacity required for market formation. Nevertheless, it is not enough to enable exchange because it does not account for the purpose of exchange. The emergence of exchange and the resulting formation of market depends on the necessity of exchange. Without the necessity of exchange, supply and payment capacity, no matter how sufficient, will not bring market behavior under the premise of bounded rationality. Such necessity of exchange, called need, is the cornerstone of market demand – need for payment capacity. Therefore, need plays a decisive role in market formation.

A classic case from the earliest market activities is the exchange of two axes for a sheep. In this case, the two parties of exchange have direct needs for the commodities of the other. Exchange will not happen if either party does not need the other's commodities. The sheep farmer chooses to exchange because he needs stronger fences to scale up farming. If he already has enough axes, exchange will not succeed even if the other party is willing to provide more axes. In the modern economy, need plays a more decisive role as consumers face multiple options. A consumer buys a product out of consideration to certain life, social, and even psychological needs. Taking bags for example, new buyers purchase the product for use. Holders purchase new or high-end products for substitution purpose and psychological satisfaction. For large possessors of high-end bags, the buying behavior basically meets the psychological need of a hobby.

(2) Need is fundamentally the source of all economic activities, including supply. All human activities of understanding and transformative nature are carried out to meet the needs of their material and cultural life. Marx (1844) noted that human need, i.e., human nature, is the motivation and basis for human beings to engage in production activities and form social relations. For human beings, "the extent that they need is the extent they produce." In other words, human needs are the motive power of their participation in labor and production. Before the exchange occurs, the quantity and scope of items produced by individuals are based on their own direct needs (and will not exceed them). The need for exchange arises as the surplus of products appear, giving rise to social relations, such as, division of labor and cooperation. Furthermore, after basic needs are met, people can "create history" and a series of historical activities will

follow. Therefore, need is the initial impetus to both social relations and historical activities. Since need is the source of production activities, demand as a manifestation of need in the market becomes a prerequisite for market formation.

Need is undoubtedly the initial driving force of human history. The boundaries of production activities defined by needs form the basic norms that underpin the modern economy. Due to obstacles in information exchange, the quantity and variety of production are always different from need. In industrial capitalism, products are manufactured in large quantities and market surplus becomes inevitable. Economic activities ignore demand, considering that supply can create demand. In this case, supply is divorced from demand, causing large-scale overproduction. After a new economic cycle starts, the excessive inventory of the previous cycle is largely squeezed out of the market because of moral depreciation (substitution effect brought by new products), though partially digested. Neither market equilibrium nor rational resource allocation is achieved. Instead, a lot of resources are wasted. This process of market operation is enough to illustrate the hazards of neglecting demand.

(3) In general market behavior after the formation of market economy, demand decides whether supply can awaken demand and ultimately leads to trading behavior. Often, supply awakens demand. For example, a new product such as a piano or car (relative to a horse-drawn carriage) can arouse demand for such products and facilitate the formation of new consumer markets and even new spending

habits. With this intuitive understanding, people simply think that supply creates demand. Even some economists believed that production could create the purchasing power of the same value as these products: supply can create its own demand.[1] Though revised and refined many times, this idea remains unable to account for economic crises frequent in the capitalist world and therefore incurs criticism from economists such as Sismondi, Malthus and Kay Burns. This theory fails because it neither proves that the consumer side has sufficient payment capacity nor indicates whether the payment capacity can be moderately allocated among people with consumption needs. Moreover, it does not find that the market is decided by demand instead of supply. The fundamental decisive power of demand lies in the true need for product, rather than adequate payment capacity.

(4) In the process of market economic activities, the quantity, value, and even production process of products supplied are determined by demand. Even if adapted to people's needs, supply often seems to exceed demand in the market due to payment constraint. The surplus will be stuck in the market and through long-term accumulation eventually lead to financial crisis. In this regard, Marx pointed out that all products can be sold only when they are produced in the necessary proportions. The quantitative limit for the proportions of social labor time in each special production field manifests further development of the entire value law. Obviously, the necessary labor time herein has another meaning. In order to meet social needs, only such labor

time is necessary. Hereon, the excess supply is abandoned by demand – only the supply realizable for social demand can be used. Thus, demand requires that production process factors including technology are consistent with consumer needs. For example, when choosing agricultural products, consumers prefer green products to products with excessive pesticide residues.

In short, the market is formed based on the existence of both demand and supply. However, it is demand that ultimately decides the realization of trading behavior and enables the true formation of market. Such demand is decided by needs instead of payment capacity. Historically, the emergence of new products, such as pianos and cars, induced need and contributed to exchange. With the maturity of the mass consumption society, whether a new product can meet demand in the market depends on whether the product successfully fills the product gap or replaces existing products to better satisfy consumer needs. It can be said that need is the ultimate determinant of market formation. Even after the establishment of market system, the market is ultimately determined by demand.

4.2 Invisible Hand: Expectations

In the market mechanism theory, price has always been regarded as the "invisible hand" in resource allocation. In actual market behavior, however, price has lost its proper directing function.

The demand for many commodities is no longer abated by rising prices or stimulated by declining prices. On the country, both demand and supply shrink as the price falls, and expand as the price rises. In addition, there is a growing tendency to deplete social resources. The scarcer the resources, the higher the prices and the more they are used. The more abundant the resources, the lower the prices and the more they are neglected and left idle. The reality of market activities proves that taking price as the "invisible hand" is a simple and superficial theoretical imagination.

Then, what is the "invisible hand" that really allocates resources in the market? Interestingly, an identical factor fundamentally decides the relationship between market supply and demand of ordinary goods. Since market formation is determined by need, this factor must first arouse demand. An observation of market behavior finds the fundamental force that determines market operation is the Expectation of market participants on the demand and supply sides. Expectations herein refer to prejudgments on benefits that can be achieved through next-stage market behavior – demand satisfied or supply realized – made under the premise of bounded rationality by the individual and social market players formed. Among them, the Expectations of consumers include the degree of satisfaction occurring at next-stage consumer utility and the availability of benefits; additionally, the Expectations of producers mainly concentrate on the expected profitability of next-stage supply.[2]

Expectations decide market operation according to the following basic mechanism: The Expectations of consumers arouse demand, which affects producers and thereby triggers supply Expectations. The Expectations of consumers refers to the expectations flowing from higher consumer income, which are generally broad and oriented, such as better functions or lower prices of commodities. Guided by such Expectations, suppliers expect benefits brought by demand, and present different demand solutions due to individual differences. The result is a group of different alternative products that share similarities in features and prices. Consumers may choose a product or a combination of several products based on their Expectations. Thus, price points form under the combined effect of consumers' expected benefit maximization and producers' expected profit maximization – at which the trading behavior is completed.

Expectations exert effects in various directions and forms under different market conditions. It should be reaffirmed that information asymmetry and bounded rationality of market participants are the basic preconditions of imperfect competition discussed herein.

(1) Both information and rational understanding indicate relatively balanced demand and supply of a specific commodity, sufficient supply of alternatives, and better information conductivity. In this scenario, when the price declines, consumers will expand or shift consumption. This will cut the orignally-expected expenditure and increase the consumer surplus. Conversely, when the price rises, consumers will reduce their consumption or shift to lower-priced alternatives because the orignally-expected expenditure has increased.

This tendency does not affect supply in the short run, but if it persists for a long time, producers will form the Expectations of noticeable revenue reduction, and thereby scale down the output.

In this case, price seems to play a role in adjusting market demand and supply. For this reason, traditional market theory considers price as the "invisible hand" and simply expands this special case into a universal principle. In fact, this case embodies only a special situation of imperfect competition – both supply and demand have certain rigidity. In this situation, i) Despite alternative bundles, the commodity has no lifecycle, which means it is not subject to replacement by new products at any time (they are usually not industrial products); ii) Price increase will not cause the inflow of external goods and the consequent price cuts, and price decline will not induce supply reduction in the short term; and iii) Demand stays relatively stable with no reduction or increase. A typical example is agricultural products, that is, the "damping goods" mentioned in the preceding sections. In addition, this accidental situation results from Expectations. The price trend judgment, income effect, and substitution effect are, without exception, based on the Expectations of consumers.

(2) Both information and rational understanding indicate a relatively inadequate supply of specific commodities and insufficient alternatives, while demand is moderately rigid. In this scenario, consumers will, in the expectation of rising price, purchase the commodity in advance for the

purpose of smaller expenditure. As a result, the higher the price of ordinary goods (non-Giffen goods), the more the purchases. This social phenomenon is more common for daily life products with rigid demand, such as salt, toilet paper, washing powder, and garlic. Such expectations also account for the rush of purchasing some commercial houses. By further driving up the price, the Expectations of consumers will, in the long run, stir producers' expectations of significant revenue growth and lead to production expansion. In this case, more supply can, more often than not, curb price rises and stabilizes demand. However, the housing market is reasonably unique, since it is influenced by rigid demand and capitalization of housing finance.

(3) Both information and rational understanding indicate an excess supply of specific commodities and relatively insufficient demand (usually in the context of economic depression). In this scenario, consumers with declining income will lower employment prospects. In such Expectations, they will consider the need for next-stage expenditure during consumption. Typically, they will pay no attention to non-essential items with lower prices and may shift consumption to alternatives with sharper price decline, or suspend consumption to maintain the basic needs of life in the next stage. Therefore, price decline will not stimulate consumption. For example, in the early 1990s, when the Japanese speculative bubble burst, there was a severe recession due to significant government, business, and individual debt. Consumption cannot be expanded by price

cuts of general industrial products, including such non-essentials like televisions, video recorders, and cameras, and even some consumer goods such as vegetables and fruits. In the long run, producers will lower their expectations of commodity profitability, and thereafter scale down commodity production or develop new products. This is exactly why an economic crisis is often catalyzed by the innovation of a few large and powerful enterprises, which leads to the collapse of many small and medium-sized enterprises.[3]

(4) In the market of traditional Giffen goods, such as ancient coins, old books, and art objects (especially in the case when the artists have passed away), the supply is fixed and basically expected by the market to have surplus due to scarcity-based price rigidity. However, these commodities are not the necessities of life. Therefore, only when price rises rapidly, will buyers choose to purchase these commodities in the expectation of significant returns. As a result, the higher the price, the greater the demand. Affected by this, the supply side raises the expectations of returns, and further push up the price until the demand side's expected returns are completely offset. Conversely, the commodities will be withdrawn from the market when collectors lose interest and no longer believe the purchase can bring the expected returns. Where Giffen goods become quasi-financial goods in which consumers invest for returns, the substitution effect further demonstrates the price failure. Goods with faster price rises are more demanded, and goods with lower

expected returns are substituted by goods with higher expected returns.

(5) Commodities with a financial nature, such as stocks, futures, and real estate, are not necessities of life. In such a market, the demand side behaves by investing for returns, with the expected difference between investment costs and future returns. Therefore, no matter whether supply is insufficient or excessive, demand will expand as long as the demand side considers there is an appreciation tendency and more wealth can be obtained in the next stage. As a result, the higher the price, the more the demand. The supply side will form expectations of greater returns, and therefore expand related supplies, such as issuing new shares, providing new commodity futures, or building new houses. The market operates in such cycles until monetary policy tightens to a certain extent, such as higher interest rates. The upward trend of price will not be curbed until the investment costs of the demand side increase and the foreseeable next-stage returns become zero or even negative – since it is offset by the price rise. When the price declines, buyers and sellers with different bounded rationality (including information) will have different Expectations. Some holders choose to sell these commodities to stop losses, while others choose to buy at a low price to make profits when the price rebounds. Some even choose high-price buybacks to increase the market price. However, when buyers and sellers agree that price decline is irreversible and price recovery cannot be expected, there will be large-scale sell-offs and no purchase,

and the price will drop (usually rapidly), leading to market collapse. Financial crises in history mostly fall into this category. For example, the Great Recession of the 1930s that begun in the United States and spread to Europe, the collapse of Japan's bubble economy in the 1990s, and the US subprime mortgage crisis raging the world in 2007/08.

To sum up, Expectations of next-stage returns based on bounded rationality are the decisive force of market behavior under various specific conditions in an imperfect market. This is reflected in the sale and purchase of not only Giffen goods, but also ordinary goods. Among them, the Expectations of consumers play a dominant role in market behavior; while the Expectations of suppliers lag behind and play a subordinate role.

Endnotes

1. James Mill. Commerce Defended [M]. London: Routledge Press, 1992.

2. The discussion of expectations was first presented by John Maynard Keynes. However, Keynes only saw the superficial phenomenon of expectations, such as the diminishing marginal utility at the microscopic level, and did not notice the decisive role of expectations in the market. Later, Kahneman focused more on the fact that expectations are unmeasurable in individual cases such as gambling. It can be said that expectations have never been really highlighted as a perspective for investigating market problems.

3. Individual non-marginal market behavior is also dominated by expectations. A typical example is the milk dumping incident. It is used in some of the early literature to expose the darkness and cruelty of capitalism: In the economic crisis of capitalism, milk becomes unsaleable due to sharp decline

in people's consumption level. What's worse, the process and preservation techniques are unable to ensure milk storage till the recovery of the economy and people's spending power. Capitalists would rather dump the milk than give it to the poor. This is inconsistent with marginal theory in economics. According to marginal theory, capitalists may lower the price to realize the value of surplus milk and obtain a small amount of return. Dumping milk does not make sense in current economic theory. However, it can be explained by the theory of expectations under the premise of bounded rationality. With bounded rationality, capitalists hope the market expectations of milk price stay stable for the sake of self-interest. If the price is reduced to almost zero when the milk is about to expire, people will form the expectation of lower price and wait for price cuts. Thus, the expectations of profitable price will be substituted. Milk can no longer be sold at normal and profitable prices that can offset the cost of production, which will ultimately lead to business bankruptcy. It is precisely because of the expectation of stable price that producers would rather dump the milk than give it away.

Chapter 5

Market Operation: Double-Wing Model

5.1 Single-Commodity Dynamic Model

Expectations as the real "invisible hand" decide market operation. The mechanism can be abstracted into the relationship between trading behavior and commodity-specific Expectations of consumers and suppliers in the entire economy, as shown in Figure 5–1.

Here, E is the quantity of a specific commodity expected by consumers or suppliers, and Q is the quantity of the specific commodity needed or supplied; 0 is the starting point of the two axes of quantity; and P_i (i =1, 2, ...) is the price at which the trading behavior is established.

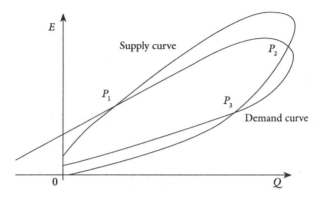

Figure 5–1 Double-wing model for single commodity

As shown in the dynamic trend of the demand and supply curves, the Expectations of consumers existed before the advent of a specific commodity. For example, consumers desired more beautiful musical instruments before the advent of piano, and more efficient means of transportation before the invention of the car. With customers' needs accumulating to a certain extent, suppliers will form the Expectations that satisfy customer needs to generate lucrative profits. Therefore, they will develop a certain product that meets demand needs. In this case, the Expectations of both consumers and suppliers are not zero but have reached a certain value when they enter the market.

Following the entry of commodities into the market, Expectations will undergo three basic stages of change:

In the first stage, consumer Expectation rises. The advent of new products meets the potential new needs of people, and the novel consumption models or habits spread in society and become fashionable. This stimulates greater and more expectations of consumers at the social level, and induces suppliers to form Expectations of profit growth and to expand production. In the case of cars, the overall profits of producers may increase as economies of scale reduce the unit price. At this stage, new consumption models continue to spread through the demonstration effect. Demand swells amid the growing expectations on purchase returns of consumers across the whole society. Supply also expands as producers raise their expectations of commodity-specific profitability. The situation is shown in P_1. However, supply increases more rapidly than demand because suppliers with rapidly growing expectations make centralized mass production, in contrast to the scattered demand of consumers.

In the second stage, the Expectations of consumers begin to shift direction. The expected capability of a specific commodity to benefit consumers weakens after a certain period of market behavior – which may be very short, and even fleeting for some products, due to the development and advent of more advanced products. Then, new Expectations of substitution arise among consumers, resulting in a general decline in Expectations at the social level. This dampens market demand and undermines producers' expectations of profitability. Subsequently, supply is reduced and production scaled down from the peak. This stage sees a turning point in the Expectations of both consumers and suppliers and an inverted U-shaped curve[1] of both demand and supply in the current and previous stages. Therefore, in the transition of Expectations of consumers, coupled with the tracking and analysis by suppliers, trading behavior may happen on occasion – the possibility of rising expectations of individual consumers and suppliers cannot be ruled out. P_2 is an example of this. It should be noted that due to time lag, P_2 may be just the point where the Expectations of suppliers and consumers are exactly equal, rather than the time they actually intersect. Since supply is dependent on demand, the turning point arrives earlier in the demand curve than the supply curve. The time lag depends on the speed and accuracy that suppliers with bounded rationality measure the decline in Expectations of consumers. It decides the amount of excess supply. Due to mass production, supply decreases faster than demand.

In the third stage, the Expectations of consumers show a steady downward trend. When a particular commodity has been impacted by new alternatives or does not appear to bring larger consumer surplus, consumers will continue to reduce the Expectations of this commodity, and raise the Expectations of new products or better alternatives. The change is fed back by way of smaller market consumption to suppliers, thereby reducing producer expectations of profitability and driving down supply. At this stage, demand shrinks as consumers lower their Expectations. Subsequently, supply decreases with the decline of the Expectations of suppliers. Like P_2, P_3 represents the point where the two curves have the same value, rather than the actual time of intersection due to time lag. Similarly, supply declines faster than demand due to mass production.

The three stages describe the commodity-specific whole process in which demand determines the generation, transition, and termination of supply. This process is reflected in the changes in market supply and demand when impacted ultimately by consumer Expectations. From the demand side, consumers form expectations, get satisfied, become bored, and expect substitutive products. From the supply side, the process is the product lifecycle. Where multiple commodities form the total social supply, new product development is interlaced. If the majority of industries lack enough new products to meet new demand and the industrial technology becomes relatively stagnant, this process forms a medium-wave economic cycle (Juglar cycle). If the entire industrial system lacks sufficient product and technological innovation to meet new demand, the process becomes a long-wave economic cycle (Kondratieff cycle).

5.2 Multi-commodity Dynamic Model

Based on the single-commodity dynamic model, the multi-commodity dynamic model can be used to further examine the complex process in which demand decides supply and supply responds to demand in the real market, as shown in Figure 5–2.

First, consumers have strong utility expectations of specific needs. The utility may be unilateral, such as the need to take photos as memory, the need to talk to the outside world for contact anytime and anywhere, the need to see or hear external information, or all of the above. The utility expectations are as shown in ① ② ③ in the first stage.

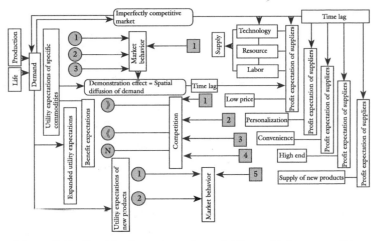

Figure 5–2 Double-plume dynamic model for multiple commodities

Then, suppliers notice the strong utility expectations of consumers, and generate profitability expectations that are sufficient to promote technological and product innovation. Thus, product ☐ that meets one or more utility needs emerges. In the preceding example, this product may be a mobile phone that meets only one of the consumer needs.

Supply ☐ meets some of the utility expectations of market demand and makes product ☐ come true. Through the demonstration effect of consumption, demand diffuses within the space that can be reached by information. The diffusion effect is transmitted with certain time lag to suppliers. It is the way that mobile phones rapidly spread in early days.

Encouraged by demand expansion, the earliest innovators and followers on the supply side further advance the competition of low-cost products through economies of scale and production process refinement, which intensifies the spatial diffusion effect of products. This satisfies consumers' income expectations based on meeting utility expectations, and greatly enhances the spatial diffusion effect of products. At this stage, despite decline in prices, the overall revenue of suppliers is significantly increased by mass production. It boosts the income expectations of suppliers and attracts more suppliers to follow up production.

With the participation of an increasing number of suppliers, products for different consumer groups come out, with an emphasis on personalization, convenience, functional improvement, and versatility. Examples include low-price products ⬚1 and personalized, convenient, and high-end products ⬚2, ⬚3, and ⬚4, as shown in Figure 5–2. The competition in supply changes from that of price into all aspects. For example, mobile phones have obviously evolved from bar phones to flip phones and further to touch-screen phones. The features have expanded from simple calls and short messages to simple cameras, high-performance cameras with increasing pixels, and further, to information platforms. Some individual brands are even known for particular sturdiness so consumers referred to these phones as "bricks."

This process enables consumers to generate the expectations of price declines and function improvement, which stimulates the advent of and substitution by new products, such as product ⬚5. In the case of mobile phones, the new product may be a full-featured AI companion robot or ultra-thin smart machine that can be folded and bent.

The above-mentioned multi-commodity dynamic model reflects the formation of heterogeneous supply induced by one or several needs of consumers and the process of market realization. In reality, the all-round needs of consumers create expectations of supply in all aspects. Therefore, this multi-commodity dynamic process appears simultaneously in each field and together forms a complete picture of real market activities.

5.3   Time Lag of Expectations

Under the actual conditions of imperfect competition, time lag exists in the impact of Expectations on market operation. It has been covered in the above-mentioned single-commodity and multi-commodity dynamic models. While the time lag in the multi-commodity dynamic model is easier to understand, the dynamic intersections of supply and demand curves in the single-commodity dynamic model are often misleading. In light of this, the time lag in different stages is explained. It can be simply summarized as a result from imperfect competition, but specific factors and impact mechanisms will be discussed in depth in the follow-up studies.

(1) Time lag for generating supply expectations

In the single-commodity dynamic model – double-wing model, consumers first have utility and price expectations, and after a period of time suppliers notice these expectations and generate expectations of profit. The period includes the time taken to notice demand and the prejudgment of suppliers on the possibility of converting expectation of need into actual goods, including technological feasibility and expectations of cost and profit. The length of time varies with the degree of attention and sensitivity of suppliers to demand expectations and supplier judgement on the market and technological feasibility. As shown in Figure 5–3, the time vector between the longitudinal axis E and the demand curve on the left can be regarded as the time lag.

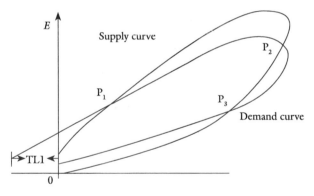

Figure 5–3   Time lag for generating supply expectations (TL1)

(2) Time lag after the expected intersection P_1

P_1 is the point where the expectations of consumers and suppliers are consistent. At this point, the price and utility expected by suppliers coincide with those provided by suppliers without compromising their profit expectations.

Therefore, this point usually signifies the start of rapid market expansion of a specific community and becomes a prelude to higher expectations of supply. However, such high expectations of supply do not accurately reflect the profits that can be brought by consumer-expected price and utility. This causes time lag between supply and demand expectations, despite the two rising synchronously with time (there is no clear time vector). In fact, it still takes time for suppliers to accurately identify consumer expectations in the market. In other words, it is for sure after a time lag that suppliers can accurately understand the content of customer expectations, as shown in Figure 5–4.

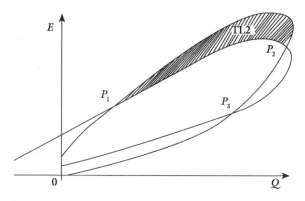

Figure 5–4 Potential time lag for understanding demand expectations (TL2)

(3) Time lag of supply expectations at the turning point of demand expectations

Due to the time lag for understanding demand expectations, supply expectations continue to rise at the moment the market changes with the reversal in demand expectations, resulting in an evident time lag of supply expectations. As shown in Figure 5–5, when the demand curve has passed the turning point and begins to fall, the supply curve continues to extend at a high level. The time lag, either long or short, has fully manifested. As a result, the intersection of demand and supply curves does not mean convergence at a particular time.

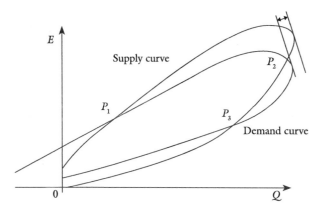

Figure 5–5 Time lag of supply expectations at the turning point of demand expectations (TL3)

(4) Time lag of supply expectations after the decline of demand expectations

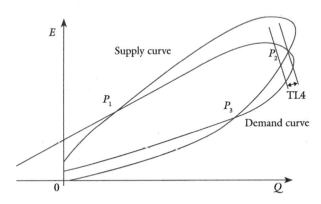

Figure 5–6 Time lag of supply expectations after the decline of demand expectations (TL4)

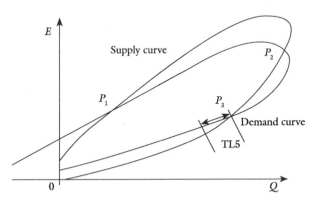

Figure 5-7 Time lag of supply expectations after the decline of demand expectations (TL5)

The turning point of supply expectations arrives at a period of time after demand expectations. This leads to time lag between demand and supply curves thereafter. The intersection at P_2 and P_3 does not imply the particular time of convergence in a real sense, but the equal value between supply and demand curves. At this particular time, the demand curve has fallen to a lower point, as shown in Figure 5–6 and Figure 5–7.

5.4 Quantitative Analysis of Expectations

Expectations are not unmeasurable. Using aggregate and statistical methods, the Expectations of social needs can be further quantified with the help of basic mathematical calculations and big data technology.

Judging from the quantitative grasp of the impact on economic activities of the entire market, Expectations are related to – but not the same as – the marginal propensity to consume (MPC). MPC refers to the proportion of additional income that an individual consumes,[2] and mainly reflects the increase of consumption elasticity with income. Although MPC indicates the propensity of consumer demand for a particular commodity, it fails to accurately grasp the propensity of consumer expectation for a particular commodity. For example, MPC cannot account for two cases: i) The overall consumption expenditure does not increase with income, but the consumption of specific commodities may expand or shrink; and ii) Despite income reduction, overall consumption expenditure increases and the consumption of specific commodities may expand or shrink. To this end, the marginal propensity of expectation is hereby introduced.

The marginal propensity to expectation of needs (MPEN) refers to the difference in the proportion of a specific commodity in the quantity purchasable by total consumption expenditure between two periods. The marginal propensity to expectation of supply (MPES) refers to the proportion of a specific commodity in the additional gross revenue of supply.

$$MPEN = C_{i(t+1)} \Big/ \Sigma C_{i(t+1)} - C_{it} \Big/ \Sigma C_{it}$$

$$MPEN = \Delta R_i / \Delta \Sigma R_i$$

Where i = 1, 2, 3. $n_0 C_i$ indicates the quantity of a specific commodity. i – bought by consumers, and Σc_i the quantity of the specific commodity. i – purchasable by additional consumption expenditure. ΔR_i is the additional revenue of producers by supplying the specific commodity i, and $\Delta \Sigma R_i$ the gross revenue of producers.

Specifically, the ability of consumers to pay for commodity A increases with income. Assuming 2 units of commodity A are bought when the total expenditure can support 10 units, if 4 units are bought when 20 units are purchasable, then MPEN is 0.2 – 0.2 = 0. This shows that consumer expectation of this commodity expands in parallel with the ability to pay. Such commodities can be called synchronous goods.

If only one unit is bought when 20 units are purchasable, then MPEN is 0.05 − 0.2 = -0.15, indicating a decline in the consumer's expectation of this commodity. If 8 units are bought when 20 units are purchasable, then MPEN is 0.4 − 0.2 = 0.2, indicating a growth in the consumer's expectation of this commodity to be higher than that of synchronous goods.

In the case of reduced overall consumption expenditure, if only one unit is bought when 5 units are purchasable in the next period, then MPEN is 0.2 − 0.2 = 0. This commodity falls into the category of synchronous goods, considering the same consumer expectation as that of the previous period. If 4 units are bought when 5 units are purchasable in the next period, then MPEN is 0.8 − 0.2 = 0.6. This shows that consumer expectation of this commodity increases and becomes much higher than synchronous goods. Of course, if the consumer gives up this commodity due to income decline, the consumer's expectation of this commodity already becomes negative and exhibits a downward trend.

In the long run, if MPEN at a certain point is greater than that of the previous period, the overall market expectation is rising, thereby driving up MPES. If MPEN at a certain point is less than that of the previous period, the overall market expectation is declining, thereby bringing down MPES. Under normal circumstances, MPEN first increases and then gradually decreases after reaching a certain peak. MEPS shows a similar trend with a certain time lag, as shown in Figure 5–8.

In short, the impact of Expectations on the market is not only fundamental and objective, but also measurable and predictable.

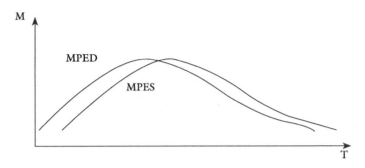

Figure 5–8 MPEN and MPES

The traditional market theory considers price as the "invisible hand" based only on the unrealistic assumption of abundant market supply and demand. If price is taken as a criterion to measure market equilibrium and corporate profit and loss, it is not difficult to find one of two possible situations: there has already been serious market imbalance once commodity prices have changed abnormally, or there has been serious overproduction when producers become aware that price cannot bring profits.

5.5 Resource Allocation with Expectations

Resource allocation is a basic function of the market. How does the market use Expectations as the "invisible hand" to allocate resources?

Demand is primary while supply is secondary. The Expectations of consumers arouse the Expectations of suppliers to provoke market behavior. In this process, resource allocation is also realized. In other words, consumers enact their Expectations through the market. Suppliers are mobilized to use appropriate resources to increase or decrease supply according to demand changes. Meanwhile, they improve the quality, features, and technological content of supply to adapt to demand upgrades, while withdrawing the supply that fails to meet said requirements. Thus, the ultimate goal of resource allocation in the market is to enable supply to fully meet demand in terms of quantity, structure, quality etc. so as to minimize resource waste and excess production, and achieve supply and demand equilibrium.

In an imperfect market, however, resource allocation through Expectations cannot completely match supply and demand. It can only get close to the optimal state of full balance and satisfaction. This can be attributed to five reasons:

(1) Information symmetry determines the accuracy of resource allocation. The demand side is unlikely to have its voice heard in all areas of production and life due to various constraints, such as the progress to a mass consumption society, the level of information technology development, and regional heterogeneity. Therefore, their Expectations are difficult to accurately convey to all areas of supply. This inevitably leads to supply behavior with Expectations based on subjective speculation and customary judgment.

(2) The bounded rationality of human understanding of nature and society determines the direction of resource allocation. On the one hand, consumers with bounded rationality are

not capable of accurately grasping their own expectations of demand. Bounded rationality, such as impulsiveness, one-sidedness, and preferences, as well as slow understanding of consumer expectation upgrades, may mislead the expectations of supply. On the other hand, suppliers may suffer waste due to the limitations of industrial technology caused by inadequate understanding of nature. They may not adopt the optimal way of supply, given the constraints of social systems (including ethics and social practices). For example, in order to meet the expectations of heating needs, suppliers have used environmentally unfriendly and unsustainable resources such as wood, coal, and oil. Even today, clean and sustainable solar energy has not been adequately applied.

(3) The mode of production determines the quantity difference of resource allocation. For a long time, the supply process has been subject to the mode of production. In agriculture, overproduction is caused by blind production due to the long production cycle and information asymmetry. In industry, overproduction is often associated with mechanized mass production. As the mass consumption society matures, consumers begin to show their power. Coupled with advances in information technology, their Expectations play a decisive role in the market in a more frequent and faster manner. This requires suppliers to adopt a flexible manufacturing system for more targeted supply.

(4) The time lag of psychological expectation transmission de-termines the efficiency of resource allocation. For a long

time, the mutual understanding of people has been challenged by information asymmetry, inadequate information transmission technologies (including information symmetry platforms), and spatial heterogeneity. Time lag is inevitable even if Expectations can be completely and accurately conveyed from demand to supply. This prolongs the cycle that the Expectations of consumers induce. As a result, the new supply that meets the latest desire of consumers is delayed, which implies excess of the old supply targeted at the earlier desire.

(5) By virtue of infinite expansion, demand is the fundamental decision-making power and the most revolutionary force in the market system. As long as humans have unlimited desires, human expectations of supply will expand indefinitely and new expectations of needs will emerge endlessly. This will inject continuous impetus to the innovation of suppliers in a constant effort to meet the expectations of consumers. This is the mechanism of development of human society, and the fundamental reason why a complete supply and demand equilibrium is achievable in a market economy.

In short, the allocation of market resources results from the impact of demand on supply. The impact exists because the Expectations of consumers affect the Expectations of suppliers. Therefore, Expectations play a decisive role.

Endnotes

1. It is referred to in some theories as the product lifecycle or the U-shaped model cattle production under environmental constraints. Examples in particular areas include the Environmental Kuznets Curve and inverted U-shaped industrial agglomeration.

2. MPC = $\Delta C/\Delta Y$, wherein C represents consumption and Y, income. Both Y and C are considered to increase in the long run.

Chapter 6

Market Trend: Imbalance and Management

6.1 Recognition of Reality: Market Imbalance

Market clearing inferred from traditional market theory has never occurred. On the contrary, there have been frequent crises of overproduction. In this regard, Western economists have conducted many discussions and generally attributed the situation to the incomplete realization of rational expectations. In fact, however, the inability of traditional market theory to explain "market failure" is caused by absurd theoretical premises.

This author believed that market imbalance is inevitable. Since there has never been a perfectly competitive market in reality, consumers and producers have only bounded rational expectations and cannot fully predict the market. It means information asymmetry is not fundamentally solved. In addition, the objective existence of space and its heterogeneity is an important reason for market imbalance.

(1) The Expectations of need are the decisive force in the market, but they can only be grasped through changes in market demand. Nevertheless, the manifestation of demand in the market is constrained by supply through purchase. Supply is also realized in the process of demand self-realization. Due to such unity of opposites and mutual establishment, demand must be realized by means of supply, while supply, bounded by rationality, tries but cannot fully meet the Expectations of needs. Hence, supply is inherently unable to accurately grasp what is really expected by demand. In addition, customers are a collection of scattered individuals, and suppliers provide centralized supply based on specialized division of labor and mode of mass production. The diversification of products in the market can increasingly meet the Expectations of vast customers. This usually conceals the real demand of customers and leads to production beyond the Expectations of needs by suppliers.

(2) Due to the bounded rationality of economic agents, both customers and suppliers are affected by their limited understanding of economics and market laws. Under certain technical conditions, the limitations on understanding of market demand are exacerbated by information asymmetry.

In particular, suppliers have limited understanding of market dynamics brought about by customer expectations. This prevents production from aligning with total market demand and adapting to the structural changes of market segments. In addition, there is always time lag in suppliers' grasp of customer expectations. Mass production enables supply to grow faster than demand. Under the combined impact, overproduction is inevitable. Besides, with the formation and upgrading of mass consumption society and changing technology, people's material and cultural needs become more and more diversified, personalized, and high-end, while production processes tend to be automated and sophisticated for mass production, making the tendency for oversupply more pronounced.

(3) Human production activities must rest on specific geographical space. Spatial limitation determines the heterogeneity of human economic activities, which further leads to market imbalance. First of all, from a historical perspective, due to spatial heterogeneity, people's needs are first met by economic factors available in a specific space, so people in the specific space have different preferences. Price guidance is not enough to fully reflect the restrictions of these preferences on supply. Spatial distance even intensifies information asymmetry and increases information search costs, making it more difficult to grasp customer expectations. Second, due to spatial heterogeneity and distance, space with geographical advantages is preferred by production activities. This creates the advantages of agglomeration that is more conducive

to the formation and expansion of economies of scale. On the one hand, economic activities drive the expansion of economies of scale, which enables supply to outstrip demand. On the other hand, economic activities catalyze monopoly by affecting supplier expectations of maximizing profits. High monopoly profits hinder innovation. As a result, old products still occupy the market for a long time after customer expectations have been satisfied, which aggravates overproduction. In addition, based on specific geographical areas with relative independence, independent administrative bodies have been historically fostered. Under the conditions of market economy, these administrative bodies, as modern states with administrative sovereignty, usually set various tariffs and non-tariff barriers for the sake of self-interest. This not only undermines the freedom of market behavior, but also restrains effective supply from satisfying regional demand, resulting in policy-based overproduction.

(4) Demand cannot be increased at the same magnitude as supply towards market clearing. First of all, the total market value of supply, reflected in the process of economic growth, has always been larger than demand. In the modern economic system, the total market price of commodity-specific supply is the sum of cost of production (including material cost and labor time cost) and surplus value of capital (profit). Among them, labor time cost is wages. As the remuneration for laborers (including producers and operators), wages are obtained after the realization of labor power as commodities, and then transformed into the payment capacity of

customers. Therefore, the payment capacity only represents a part of the total market price, and under no circumstances is it equal to or greater than total market price. Second, the wages and profits involved are not evenly distributed to each consumer. Typically, a dominant part goes to the owners of capital, and a small part to managers, mental workers, and general workers. Moreover, in the specific product market, such payment capacity will not be fully invested, which means total payment capacity in the market is far lower than total market price of supply. Besides, due to regional heterogeneity, the commodity-specific supply is not necessarily welcomed by demand in all regional markets. In other words, inherent individual characteristics of demand are often neglected by mass-produced supplies. Especially in the long historical period after the birth of a socialized production system, the Expectations of needs have been suppressed by the limited payment capacity of customers. Unable to challenge supply under existing technological conditions, customers have to succumb to the limited consumption provided by supply, and choose their goods combinations accordingly. This creates a false impression that supply meets the expectations of needs. Suppliers therefore firmly believe their products meet the needs of the market and supply can create demand.[1] Due to all these factors, combined with the above-mentioned economies of scale and monopoly, supply will eventually become more disproportionate to demand due to its blind self-confidence, leading to independent expansion and overproduction.

In short, market imbalance is bound to happen as a result of inevitable quantitative or structural overproduction. Market imbalance is used herein instead of "market failure." The economic term "market failure" describes the failure of market regulation to cajole the "free market" into the achievement of market clearing. However, analysis shows that market success is inherently impossible and has never been achieved. Hence, traditional market theory on "market failure" is methodologically unscientific.

6.2   Inevitable Choice: Market Management

Based on the theoretic premise of imperfect competition, the inevitability of market imbalance can be better understood. For this reason, the objective existence of market management is necessary.

In the development process of economic activities to date, market management has experienced four stages: self-sufficiency, laissez-faire, demand management, and supply management. In fact, even in the early stages, market was not completely unmanaged. The management of specific commodity markets (regulation of grain, salt, etc. before capitalism) and the management of international markets (trade liberalization, trade barriers, etc. in the early days of capitalism) have long existed and affected market equilibrium. Human economic activities have proved that core market management lies in supply rather than demand management.

6.2.1 Self-sufficiency

The stage of self-sufficiency represents a historical period from the formation of the early market to the emergence of the capitalist mode of mechanized mass production. As Marx said, needs are the fundamental driving force of economic activities. Driven by needs, production technologies advance step by step with difficulty, gradually meeting the material and cultural needs of people. Affected by technological progress, people's Expectations of possible market supply cannot exceed the products available at that time, despite unlimited desires for consumption. Therefore, during this stage, the Expectations of demand were mostly "basic" household items, covering food, clothing, housing, and travel, and the acquisition of simple production tools. They were met by supply through regional markets. Generally, agriculture satisfied food demand, and handcrafts met the demand for agricultural production tools and the needs of daily life. Such supply was limited in quantity and variety. With long production cycles, there was little excess supply, yet frequent shortages of food supply (due to low level of production technologies) still occurred. In light of this, the economic policy for market management focused on food supply expansion.

In the era of self-sufficiency, food was a fundamental commodity that controled the lifeline of a country. Farmers, the producers in a self-sufficient economy, relied on themselves for the supply of necessities of life, or exchanged the surplus food to meet these needs. Food as the most basic product became the core supply. There must be surplus for exchanges without compromising the most basic physiological needs. As farmers were subject to taxation, the total food supply was required to be adequate enough. Nevertheless, due to the large number of feudal lords, bureaucrats, and merchants, consumption was far beyond the scope of necessities of life, and food supply by farmers was often unable to support the total demand of society. The change of dynasties in Chinese history often manifests itself in a periodic cycle caused by inadequate food supply. At the beginning of a dynasty, governance was streamlined to stabilize the people and restore the economy. However, with the arrival of prosperity, corruption and extravagance arose; waste and encroachment caused damages; and taxation exhibited severe drawbacks. All was ultimately borne by agriculture. As a result, agricultural production faced increasing pressure. The long-standing problems, coupled with natural and man-made disasters, made it difficult for most people to survive. The dynasties ended up collapsing in either invasions or uprisings. Then, the chaos was cleared and governance was streamlined to stabilize the people... such cycles went on. The situation in Europe was no different. Therefore, a competent government of this era mainly endeavored to boost food production, and managed the supply based on rigid minimum expectations of demand.

6.2.2 *Laissez-faire*

Market management entered the laissez-faire stage as mass industrial production was established through the first industrial revolution. The first industrial revolution used the spinning jenny and steam engine as source technology.[2] While enabling the large supply of textiles, the industrial revolution drove the rapid development of transportation machinery, coal, steel, machinery manufacturing, and other industries, and the large demand and supply of related means of production. From the consumption perspective, the effect was mainly reflected in the demand for textiles. The expectations of need for textiles as necessities of life were still bounded by traditional consciousness. However, the industrialized supply quickly exceeded the quantity and quality expectation, so textile production did not need to consider the expectation of market needs. At the same time, large-scale supply was enabled under the mass production system. The scale had surpassed the regional market and would eventually shift to the global market, thus overproduction was inevitable. The expectations of needs for means of production expanded rapidly, driving the surge in related supplies. At that time, however, the direct production of consumer goods was concentrated in the textile sector, and other production and transportation sectors basically served textiles. Due to market limitations of consumer goods, overproduction was inevitable in all supplies, including means of production. Proposed in this context, traditional market principles suggested that market equilibrium can be achieved through price adjustment. The theory was constrained by the understanding of economic activities and embodied the intention to promote market expansion and guarantee capitalist production.

During this period, the government adopted a laissez-faire approach to market management. Externally, a free trade policy was implemented, which actually focused on the clearing of its own market regardless of other markets. Internally, frantic production expansion was allowed during the boom, and then excess products were naturally absorbed in the long-term recession, until the new economic recovery restarted a new cycle of overproduction. Hence, both in theory and in policy, market management centered on the interests of supplying the bourgeoisie, and focused on the realization of supply while ignoring the decisive role of demand. Of course, market clearing was never possible in terms of the overall market.

As the second industrial revolution used electric power, internal combustion engines, and petroleum as source technology, the new supply of automobiles, electric lights, and telegraphs completely transformed daily life, and drove forward the process of urbanization in all respects. The mass consumption society begun to take shape. Consumer expectations were greatly stimulated and raised, and the new supply was quickly realized on the market. Traditional market theory that favors the achievability of market clearing seemed to be proved in reality. Nevertheless, overproduction was unavoidable due to the mode of mass production. Contradictions gradually accumulated amid global market competition and arguably led to largescale warfare, such as, World War I and World War II.

6.2.3. Demand Management

Demand management began after the end of World War II. In the aftermath of two painful wars, management economics represented by Keynesianism became greatly favored. (Keynesian economics was also adopted by President Roosevelt in the

1930s following the Great Recession) However, in traditional economics, Keynesianism does not recognize demand as the primary driving force. Keynesians attributed the economic crises to the insufficiency of effective demand, and therefore, adopted demand management.

With the advent of the third industrial revolution, which used industrial technology such as microelectronics as the source technology, market supply further penetrated every aspect of people's lives, and the mass consumption society began to mature. In terms of supply, a wide range of products came out, such as radios, washing machines, refrigerators, televisions, computer-based office machines, and industrial robots. They not only replaced traditional consumer goods in daily life, but also gradually realized the substitution of daily labor and production. The increase in the variety, scale, and quality of these supplies facilitated the maturity of mass consumption. In terms of demand, people's payment capacity increased along with economic growth. Although the overall capacity of demand remained lower than the overall price of supply, structural adjustments can be made in specific industries and fields of product to proactively guide supply. Meanwhile, people were no longer satisfied with popular products with unified styles and functions. They began to display heterogeneous needs and select products that reflect personal consumption. In this context – in the market economy following the Second World War – demand became associated with economic growth and proactively guided supply. Driven by demand, supply was comprehensively upgraded and gradually diversified, personalized, and improved.

During this period, the government adopted Keynesian demand management and mainly applied it to market management during economic crises. The so-called demand management did not cover all effective demand or all of the demand, but only part of the demand in a specific period of a crisis. In general, government-led public investment stimulated related demand in the market, with a view to mitigating the crisis through the multiplier effect. Therefore, demand management was highlighted by policy makers as an effective crisis response and maintained thereafter. But in fact, since the mass consumption society, demand has accumulated power to drive supply changes. Supply management has employed marketing channels at the corporate level to explore demand trends, and made adjustments and improvements increasingly according to market demand. Such change provides a useful step in the transition of market management from emphasis on demand to supply after the 1990s.

6.2.4 Supply Management

Supply management represents a more advanced stage of market management. The approach is oriented to market demand and aims at meeting the material and spiritual needs of people. For a long time, the decisive role of demand in economic activities has been ignored, to a certain extent, by traditional market theory, serving capital and concealed by limited information technology. The market mechanism has been artificially described as a process in which supply determines demand or supply and demand jointly determine the market. However, with the progress of productivity and the upgrading of people's consumption structure, the decisive role of demand in economic activities will gradually manifest in the middle and advanced stages. Demand will become the material basis for the institutional design of on-demand production.

Supply management differs from Keynes' effective demand management, which is mainly used to deal with the impact of economic crises. On the one hand, supply management can be widely applied to various stages in the economic cycle. On the other hand, such targeted supply management is embodied in the business activities of enterprise, such as production, technological innovation, and marketing, as well as in the refined management functions of government.

Supply management does not center on the blind transformation of production, but on the predictive and precise innovation, adjustment, and upgrade according to the Expectations of needs and demand. The emergence of supply management rests on two basic premises: i) Social demand is strong enough to demonstrate heterogeneous and forward-looking Expectations and force supply to pay attention to these demand trends; and ii) The revolutionary development of information technology is sufficient to support consumers in reflecting their Expectations in a quick, concrete, and direct manner. Under these two premises, supply management directly targeted at demand firstly triggers the transformation of enterprise market behavior patterns in the production field. The reasons are as follows:

(1) As social demand grows beyond the stage of mass consumption, the Expectations of entire social demand are no longer satisfied with the supply of products. They begin to directly show heterogeneity, such as personalized needs, different specifications, and diverse features. At this stage, people's capacity for demand increases along with economic growth, but the overall payment capacity is still less than the overall price of the market supply, hindering the realization of overall market clearing. Nevertheless, as the mass consumption society develops to a certain extent, demand has accumulated sufficient power in specific areas of supply in developed and more developed regional markets. It can reflect the inherent heterogeneity and advancement of individual consumer expectations of needs through the screening and selection of market supply. This tendency emerged in the late 1980s, but developed slowly. Production activities guided by the Expectations of consumers were not expanded until big data and Internet technologies became widespread in the early 21st century. In such industries as clothing, daily necessities, and automobiles, flexible production systems are geared towards customized smart manufacturing.

(2) Rapidly developing modern information technology fully guarantees and supports the quick, concrete, and direct transmission of consumer expectations to suppliers by providing sufficient and effective technical means. This enables suppliers to fully understand the Expectations of needs for specific products, including product features, specifications,

and styles, and encourages suppliers to change production plans, reform technologies, and even adjust industrial systems. Since the information technology revolution of the 1990s, the Internet has quickly spread across the world's major economies and continues to expand. Owning to such advancement in information technology, a sufficient number of consumers have been enabled to convey and express Expectations. A variety of industries have been boosted, such as e-commerce, Internet of Things, and information services. Information platforms directly contacting the production and consumption sides have sprung up, which facilitates the transmission of consumer expectations of specific products. In addition, by integrating information technology, flexible production systems have been established to support intelligent production, and therefore suppliers can timely adjust the mode of supply according to consumer expectations.

Meanwhile, with the formation of mass consumption, rapid development of information technology, and a highly conscious social civilization, a dynamic model of targeted supply management can be further fostered. Hence, government-led market management actively shifts from simple regulation of effective demand in response to economic crises to supply management at a higher stage – proactive adjustment of the supply system based on the grasp of Expectation needs, so as to manage operations within the whole economic cycle. Efforts are made to help suppliers more accurately grasp the market, so as to adjust the quantity and structure of social supply according to social demand. Especially, given the rapid advancement of modern information technology, the dynamic grasp of structural upgrades in demand will be more convenient and accurate. This makes it easier for supply to meet the demand, and thereby directs supply towards on-demand production. However, close attention should be paid to group needs for environmental protection and resource sustainability, to consciously guide cleaner production and resource conservation in social supply, ensuring the sustainability of economic activities across society.

6.2.5 Market Management in the Future

With the extensive and in-depth application of information technology in economic life, information asymmetry in the market will be greatly alleviated. Under the premise of bounded rationality, the supply through blind production to meet Expectations of demand will be substantially reduced, and the self-regulation of market will begin to produce effects. Accordingly, the government will change its role in market management and focus its policies on the three main fields of supply management.

(1) Market information asymmetry will be addressed by vigorously building platforms that support information symmetry. These platforms should fully indicate the Expectations of demand and demonstrate technical capabilities of supply to the maximum extent. Only in this way can suppliers un-

derstand the direction of demand and achieve on-demand production without repetitive and excess production.

(2) Public supply management will be undifferentiated to ensure demand in favor of sustainable social development. Even if information symmetry is greatly enhanced, the difference in quantity and structure between market supply and demand will always exist despite gradual reduction. In view of this, the reuse of excess products is important for sustainable social development, and the circular economy should be integrated as an important part of public policy. Since resource and environmental sustainability is a basic need of human survival, public policy on resources and the environment should be gradually adjusted and deepened. In addition, education, medical care, and health should be included in the scope of supply management.

(3) Economic security policy that sustains the country's survival cannot be abandoned. In particular, the stable and sound development of the grain industry and major basic industries should not be ignored in supply management. In the current era, these industries present smaller revenue, longer production cycles, slower technological progress, and relatively insignificant market regulation, compared with consumer goods. Nevertheless, these industries are essential to the national economy and people's wellbeing. Before the arrival of relative market equilibrium, appropriate support should be given to these industries, in order to ensure national economic security and create a stable environment for the entire market.

Endnotes

1. The theory that supply creates demand fails because it does not recognize these facts: i) Consumers in the market do not have sufficient payment capacity; ii) The payment capacity is not reasonably distributed among groups with consumption needs; iii) Demand is the determinant of market, in which fundamentally, people's needs for specific commodities has the decisive force, rather than adequate payment capacity.

2. Source technology refers to pioneering major innovative technologies that induce industrial revolutions. For related content, please refer to Zhao Ruyu. Theory of Industrial Revolution [M]. Beijing: Science Press, 2003; Zhao Ruyu, From Damage to Harmony A Study of the Evolution of Industrial Technology System of Northeast China [M]. Changchun: Jilin University Press, 2005.

Chapter 7

Demand: The Market Decider

In the aftermath of the 2008 financial crisis, countries all over the world turned to supply management in unison. This stemmed from the inability of the existing production system to adapt to the upgraded demand structure. It is essentially a demand-oriented supply adjustment strategy that conforms to the market mechanism. It suggests government market management approaches have advanced beyond the Keynesian principle of effective demand.

7.1 Return of Demand as the Decider

As mentioned earlier, demand is the primary determinant of market establishment and even market operation; supply arises from demand and makes sense because of its existence; both the scale and structure of supply are subject to demand. In the process of market operation, supply cannot create demand. On the contrary, there is inevitably a tendency of overproduction. Therefore, supply needs to be aware of demand expectations and adhere as close as possible in quantity, type and structure. Only then can relative market equilibrium be achieved and massive overproduction avoided.

However, since the birth of classical economics, the decisive role of demand in the market has not been fully recognized. A succession of theories that emphasize the decisive role of supply have emerged, such as production advantages based on: labor time, division of labor, and factor endowments. Even worse, Say's law disseminates that "supply creates its own demand." Influenced by these theories, the market economy of the industrialized age has served the bourgeoisie from the start and is guided by capitalist profits.

Adam Smith (1776) fully respected supply. In his theory, price is determined by supply in the form of labor time. Market clearing is the full realization of supply, which seems to have no connection with whether demand is fully satisfied. Market is a game between supply and demand. When there is a positive difference between the actual demand and supply in the market, the market price will be higher than the natural value of the commodity; otherwise, the market price will be lower. The optimal allocation of resources is the flow of resources between supply sectors under the effect of price – an invisible hand. Free competition has resulted in a unified profit margin among various sectors, which means that supply and demand are in equilibrium and the market clears.

Furthermore, the basic principle of the international division of labor is also determined by supply – a country with an absolute advantage in labor time of producing a certain commodity can participate in the international division of labor of this commodity.

The following economists have inherited this respect for supply. David Ricardo (1817) developed the theory of comparative advantage on the basis of Adam Smith's theory, to cover up the academic limitations of the latter in advocating free trade specifically for the United Kingdom – that is, even if a country does not have an absolute advantage, it can also participate in the international division of labor with its comparative advantage to save labor.

Bertil Ohlin (1933) went further by proposing the factor endowment theory, which directly stated that the cause of the international division of labor lies in factor endowments on the supply side.[1] He believed the demand and desires of consumers, the ownership of production factors affecting personal income and even demand, and the supply of production factors together determine the supply and demand relationship, and thereby determine the price difference. Ohlin also claimed that while different demand conditions have an impact, sometimes huge regional differences in production factors can be decisive. The assumption that production factors (except land) have the same proportions in all commodities is very important to this theory and cannot be ignored in any amendment. In this way, Ohlin ruled out the influence of other factors, except the supply of production factors (factor endowments), to establish the resource endowment theory. Ohlin's theory contains a logic error – the premise of his theory ignored the difference in demand and productivity among countries. It was later criticized by Leontief (1953, 1956) through empirical test. Nevertheless, the resource endowment theory still occupies an important academic position, while Leontief's falsification became known as the Leontief Paradox.

Keynes's (1936) theory of effective demand is a tremendous improvement over classical theory, but the starting point is still supply-centric.[2] Keynes called the point of intersection of aggregate demand and aggregate supply – function effective demand. Effective demand depends on the decisions of manufacturers to maximize profits, and determines output and employment of social equilibrium. It is insufficient effective demand that causes underemployment. The reasons behind insufficient effective demand can be analyzed in aspects of consumption and investment. The root lies in three basic ideas of people: diminishing marginal propensity to consume, diminishing marginal efficiency of capital, and liquidity preference. However, only on the premise that manufacturers maximize profits, is demand brought by supply-determined employment deemed as effective demand. Therefore, even though Keynes disavowed the market mechanism at the heart of classical economics, he still give priority to the interests of the supply side.

As the economic practice of humans deepens, the supply-first mindset has gradually shown its theoretical limitations. The market has begun to reveal its true face – demand is the primary determinant. People are required to take the initiative to shift the market management model from laissez-faire and effective demand management based on supply, to supply management based on demand.

Supply adjustment is proposed, based on the contradiction between the demand of the world market (including the Chinese market) and the supply of the Chinese production system. Enterprise needs to make use of technological upgrades and innovation to meet these new demands. It can be seen that supply management is essentially demand-oriented scale adjustment and structural upgrade of supply. It is an active industrial policy adopted to resolve market imbalance through the construction of new industrial system.

7.2   Demand Development Process

As mentioned earlier, the market is bound to be out of balance, so market management is essential. Respect for the law of the market is not to allow self-regulation of the market, but to conduct necessary management in accordance with market law. Since market is determined by demand, respect for the law of the market implies respect for demand and production on demand. When supply deviates from demand, managing supply oriented to demand represents the greatest respect for the law of the market. Market management so far has given free rein to supply or fueled demand by supply, both of which violate the internal law of the market, unlike supply-side reform.

Demand is need that has the ability to pay. The need or desire of people is boundless, but not the ability to pay. Even if there are a handful of billionaires, their spending power is confined, which is reflected in the ultimately limited market demand of the whole society. Especially in the early stage of industrialization, the decisive role of demand in the market had not manifested.

In the economic stage of self-sufficiency, the most important goods were basic daily necessities such as food and clothing, and the peasant class, which accounted for the majority of society, was self-sufficient. Therefore, social consumption was effectively disadvantaged in the market. In most cases, supply, especially of food, was insufficient. In the face of insufficient food, demand was self-evidently humble.

After the first industrial revolution, the supply of industrial products represented by textiles increased substantially. However, due to capitalist exploitation, consumer ability to pay was still very weak. Capitalist countries such as Great Britain were busy carving up the world market and even waged wars to solve overproduction. The supply side produced without restraint for the benefit of capitalists, allowing overproduction and addressing it through the cycle. In this period, of course, demand was not respected at all.

After the second industrial revolution, cars and other large consumer goods gradually arose. Industrial workers expanded rapidly in scale along with speedy urbanization, providing the market with a large population of needs. People's potential demands were being met one by one, despite few alternative options. The need of clothing became ordinary and simple, with a wide variety of textiles available at various prices. Owning to breakthroughs in electric power technology, modern electric power supplies such as electric lights, telegraphs and telephones enriched people's daily lives and met their needs for information and communication. The emergence of automobiles offered a new option of travel in addition to bicycles and horse-drawn carriages. New urban life was becoming the mainstream lifestyle of the masses, and diverse daily necessities were emerging in an endless stream… In the face of new lifestyles, demand was given few alternative options, but driven by supply. Supply seemed to be creating its own demand. And capital was proudly satisfied with the rich benefits of the new supply.

The third industrial revolution following the Second World War, with microelectronics and other industrial technologies as source technology, enabled market supply to further penetrate people's lives. The mass consumption society began to mature. In the field of supply, radios, washing machines, refrigerators, televisions, computer-based office machinery, and industrial robots came out one after another. They not only replaced traditional consumer goods, but also gradually realized the substitution of daily labor and production labor. In the field of demand, however, people's ability to pay rose with economic growth. Although aggregate demand remained lower than aggregate supply price, the capability to actively guide supply through restructuring formed in specific industries and specific product areas. On the other hand, people's needs could no longer be satisfied by popularized products with uniform styles and functions, and began to show heterogeneous characteristics. Products that reflect consumer personality and meet specific needs were chosen. Against this backdrop, the market economy in the aftermath of the Second World War saw the following changes: demand moved toward socialization along with economic growth and began to actively guide supply; supply improved all round and became gradually diversified, personalized, and high-end from demand stimulation.

In the 21st century, the industrialized and urbanized model of life created during the second industrial revolution has slowly matured. In particular, the information technology revolution led by the United States has significantly enhanced market information symmetry. Large comprehensive supply has expanded with the rise of developing countries, greatly increasing the selectivity of demand. Also, people's demand structures have evolved with the increase in per capita income. Although aggregate demand is still far from clearing the supply, demand has enough power to refuse certain kinds of goods or to express unique preference or pickiness. Demand has begun to gradually show its decisive effect on the market.

Demand has a fundamental role in the market, but in reality, this decisive role has been suppressed by supply for a long time. Some economists have even claimed that supply creates its own demand. Yet, the decisive role of demand is realized only after the market economy has developed to a certain level. This involves three basic conditions, described as follows:

First, mass consumption has reached maturity. The expectations of consumers grow with people's income and consumption levels. The demand expectations of society are no longer limited to large quantities of products with uniform specifications and functions. They begin to prefer differentiated products, and even seek advanced supply beyond existing technological capacity. Personalized demand requires the continuous shift of supply to the direction of multiple specifications. High-end demand requires the improvement of product quality, the increase of added value of consumption, and the enhancement of multifunctional and intelligent products. The demand for convenience requires products that are easy to use, operate, and handle, and the transfer from supply to demand is fast and comprehensive.

Second, from the perspective of supply, social production has also reached a certain height. For specific demand, market supply is no longer singular. There is enough differentiated supply to provide the demand side with relatively sufficient alternatives. Additionally, production capacity has formed for the supply of products that can be substituted. On this basis, due to the choice of demand, the potential production capacity of a certain supplier may rapidly expand and completely replace the production capacity of other suppliers.

Third, information symmetry between the supply and demand sides has reached a certain level. The personalized, high-end, and convenience requirements of demand can be quickly, accurately and widely spread to the majority of relevant individuals. Such information symmetry was beyond imagination before Internet technology became popular in the world's major economies. However, in the post-2010 process of global economic development, developed economies in Europe, the United States, and Japan, and emerging economies such as China have attached great importance to Internet Plus as a critical area of post-crisis industrial revolution. Market information symmetry has developed at a surprisingly fast pace thereafter. The huge success in this technical field has created sufficient technical conditions for giving demand the decisive role in the market and for demand to determine supply.

Under the above three conditions, demand gradually strengthened its mechanism of influence on supply, evolving from choosing alternative products to intervening in the supply process.

Influencing supply by choosing alternative products is a basic and relatively simple way that demand determines supply. When aggregate supply is small with few alternative products available, the demand side fully reflects the inclination of expectations through strong purchases, thereby stimulating the expansion of aggregate supply and the presentation of new and alternative products by competitors. Therefore, the demand side further chooses alternative products to realize its impact on supply: i) The selection of personalized products reflects consumption preferences; ii) The selection of multi-functional and high-end products reflects consumption structure upgrade; iii) The selection of pollution-free and nuisance-free products reflect the pursuit of health and sustainable development; and iv) The selection of convenient, safe, and thoughtful methods of service reflects the extended demand for consumption process. When information technology is not fully developed, the above-mentioned expression of demand expectations can be realized only through the market information feedback of manufacturers. This results in a slow and inefficient process. When information technology is mature enough to improve market information symmetry, foot voting from the demand side can truly exert its decisive power. The successful supply sought after by demand produces the same demonstration effect as the failed supply abandoned by demand. It immediately attracts attention from the market and is used as reference.

At the same time, with the support of Internet technology, the business-to-consumer (B2C) platform for direct dialogue between businesses and consumers has been widely established, making it possible to customize supply to demand. The intervention of demand in supply is embodied not only in the customization of product functions, but also in the involvement in the entire production process from design to manufacturing and sales. In China, the demand for clothing, furniture, household appliances, agricultural products, and other fields is gradually exerting a decisive effect on supply. Hence, the impact of demand on the market has entered a new stage. The mode of action of demand has changed from affecting the realization of existing products to affecting the evolution of production processes. It speeds up the development of social production towards on-demand production, and will play an important role in changing market imbalance.

In short, the expectations of demand employ information technology to facilitate the transmission of market information. This gradually prompts supply to consciously form its own expectations based on demand expectations. The demand-based independent management of supply-side individuals is a conscious behavior with enterprises as the main entities. It can gradually merge into social forces and change market management models in the entire economy. In addition, with mass consumption and the leap in information technology, a dynamic and precise supply management model can be fostered with high social awareness, implemented by the government to meet social needs. Subsequently, government-led market management has also proactively shifted from simply mobilizing effective demand to responding to economic crises.

7.3   New Demand Calling for New Supply

To achieve on-demand production, supply management is necessary. The ultimate goal of current supply management is to build a new industrial system with the ability to meet demand from the perspective of productivity.

The new industrial system must meet not only the local or national demand, but also the related demand of the world market. Such demand includes traditional life demand and emerging personalized, high-end and convenience demand,

and covers the demand of individuals as consumers and the public demand of social groups. The industrial systems so far have satisfied people's demand from low to high, but all face the challenge of structural upgrade and product innovation. Industrial innovation driven by new industrial revolution is needed to address newly expressed demands. Meanwhile, the sustainable development strategies of group demands require greening the entire industrial system. This will fundamentally change the way energy and resources are used, and make the reconstruction of the entire industrial system more meaningful.

First, the industrial system formed since the second industrial revolution should be reshaped. This involves two main tasks: i) Transform traditional industries with informatization, automation, and intelligentization; and ii) Use electric vehicles, new energy and materials to replace unsustainable parts in the system – that is traditional industrial sectors such as automobiles, oil and steel. Second, in order to meet the demand for human health and aging population, as well as the new demand for personalization and convenience, industrial innovation in health, Internet Plus and other industrial fields should be encouraged.

Endnotes

1. Bertil Ohlin: Interregional and International Trade.

2. Keynes, J. M. The General Theory of Employment, Interest and Money [M]. London: Macmillan, 1936:2.

Chapter 8

Expectation Mechanism: The Role of Big Data

The market operates through the expectation mechanism. By fully grasping demand expectations, supply can be managed to maximize the propensity to on-demand production. The realization needs the help of advanced information technology. The advent of big data will greatly change market information asymmetry. As a result, the demand expectations of consumers will be gradually revealed and become increasingly copious, which is convenient for suppliers to scope and for policy decision-makers to predict – an era of demand-oriented precision supply management has arrived.

8.1 Dawn of the Big Data Era

The era of big data has quietly arrived amid the rapid development of Internet and information technologies. Big data is characterized by volume, velocity, variety, value and veracity. It includes all the data in processing and analysis, which excels the conventional data collection approach of random sampling. This is of epoch-making significance for analysis, forecasting, and management in social, economic, and other aspects based on massive data. In March 2012, the United States took the lead in launching big data research. In May 2016, it published the Federal Big Data Research and Development Strategic Plan, proposing to establish a big data innovation ecosystem. With the support of big data technology, the plan explores the important role of massive data in economic activities, so as to facilitate better decision analysis and strategic deployment for future economic and social development. The UK established the Open Data Institute; France released the Digital Roadmap; Japan unveiled the ICT Comprehensive Strategy Towards 2020; and South Korea announced the Smart Seoul 2015 Initiative... The major countries of the world have integrated one after another into the era of big data to seize the preemptive opportunities of development.

Below the level of national strategy, industrial development and business practices have also seen the increasingly extensive application of big data technology. For example, the Billion Prices Project proposed by MIT economists calculated daily inflation indexes based on online retail transaction data, and successfully predicted the decline in aggregate social demand, two months earlier than the official statistics for the same period. This evidently demonstrates the nowcasting capability of this technology. In this sense, big data as a service based on massive information analysis and forecasting has huge potential of application in economic regulation and market management. It will improve government decision-making on economic activities and further assist sustainable social and economic development. This chapter looks into the specific ways that big data applies to social and economic activities, and contributes to sound economic development through supply management.

The application of big data can fundamentally solve market information asymmetry. It thereby makes precise social supply management possible. Herein, planning is the method of economic operation, and market is the mechanism underpinning economic activities. The two can coexist to better guide social and economic practices. Through massive data acquisition, analysis, and processing, decision makers can more accurately grasp market demand and allocate resources to fields in real need – as reflected in demand expectations – so that on-demand production can be gradually actualized. This novel mode of market operation paves the foundation for precise supply management in the new era. For example, massive datasets facilitate economic nowcasting and propel mass customization, thereby promoting social progress and sustainable economic development.

8.2 Big Data and Traditional Economic System Reform

The application of big data is of great significance to operation mode reform of the current economic system. The choice of taking the traditional path of economic development by major countries and regions mainly falls on the dispute between market economy and planned economy. Historically, the two paths, each with pros and cons, spurred social and economic development within certain periods while exhibiting inevitable practical drawbacks. The emergence of big data technology has just pointed the way for future economic reform.

As traditional theories of market economy become ineffective in practical application, more and more scholars are probing the underlying operation mechanism of market economy. It is believed that demand plays a decisive role in market establishment, while the expectations of market players serve as the fundamental driving force of market operation. Firstly, demand takes shape through consumer expectations, and brings about supply through producer expectations. Consumer expectations of maximum utility meet consumer expectations of maximum profits at the price point to complete the transaction behavior. In short, expectations first generate demand and then induce supply, and market activities arise from this. Hence, if we can understand the fluctuations of demand from the source of expectations, we will be able to fundamentally grasp market dynamics, predict the behaviors of market players, and achieve information symmetry to the largest extent.

Under the premise of information symmetry, the planned economy can utilize its advantages fully to avoid overproduction and economic crisis. It should be noted that planning is the means and method of resource allocation rather than the operating mechanism. Therefore, it is not antagonistic but subordinate to the market economy. We need to dissolve the notion "planning is opposed to market" and stop viewing them as mutually exclusive. In essence, all economic activities are carried out in the context of market economy. Demand determines market establishment and stems from expectations. Based on symmetrical information in a market economy, planned resource allocation can attune production activities more to social needs. Hence, central planning is not contradictory to the market as the mechanism behind economic activities.

The application of big data technology realizes maximum information symmetry. Specifically, through the acquisition, analysis, and processing of massive data of expectations, enterprise can keep track of real-time market demand to develop a more accurate and detailed production plan. Based on a large amount of production data collected from enterprise, the government can control the direction of supply management at the macro level, and allocate social resources in a planned way to areas of real need, truly realizing on-demand production. This bottom-up model of supply management has obvious advantages in grasping market demand dynamics compared with the past top-down approach of central planning. It prevents economic crisis by fundamentally resolving the problem of overproduction in the traditional economic operating system.

In general, big data technology actively adjusts supply by grasping demand expectations, and catalyzes the transition of market management from simple mobilization of effective demand to on-demand supply at a higher stage. On this basis, the concept of data-based precision social supply management is proposed. Precise supply management is an advanced stage of market management centered on the market mechanism, and social management is the collection of individual (enterprise) self-management. In fact, the planned economy that appeared under a specific social system at a particular historical period is the social supply management performed by state actors. Only in a highly conscious social civilization, is it possible to achieve social management performed by the state.

8.3 Important Role of Big Data in Precise Supply Management

The big data revolution provides a material basis for on-demand production. It guarantees and supports, by sufficient and effective technical means, the expectations of demand can be quickly and directly transmitted to supply, prompting the supply side to change production plans, reform production technologies, and even adjust industrial systems. The current application of big data technology in precise supply management is mainly embodied in the following aspects:

8.3.1 *Provide opportunities for economic nowcasting*

Data prediction and analysis is an important foundation and technical guarantee for precise supply management. However, data acquisition has not been synchronized with economic development for a long time. In addition to a large time lag, it is subject to repeated revisions. As a result, traditional economic forecasting and policy making have always used past data to predict present and future development. The prediction of the present is highly accurate but not meaningful, while the prediction of the future is inaccurate due to the long time interval. For example, gross domestic product (GDP) is a key indicator in macroeconomics. This month's data can be known next month at the earliest, and this year's data may be released at least half a year later. In other words, relying on traditional methods of statistical analysis, we would not be able to know the current economic activities in a timely manner. With the integration of big data technology, nowcasting as an emerging economic analysis technique can effectively compensate this deficiency.

Nowcasting, a word derived from meteorology, is originally a reconnaissance method that uses a large amount of data from short time series in a specific region to forecast weather conditions, such as thunderstorms and typhoons. When extended to economics, it refers to the speculation based on available information with regard to matters that may have happened – where the exact situation is difficult to know precisely because of information unavailability.[1] For example, for predicting GDP of this month, GDP has already been created, but the relevant data is not available (at this time). Using big data technology, the GDP data in the first two weeks of this month can be obtained for prediction. Nowcasting is aimed at key indicators of economic development that are less frequently collected and hardly accessible. It is conducted by modeling based on easily accessible, closely related high-frequency data. Taking GDP (an important indicator reflecting the level of economic development of a country or region) as an example, data is generally released on a quarterly basis, long after the end of each quarter. In this case, the large amount of monthly data and even weekly data of relevant indicators, such as, the industrial production index, product sales, and added manufacturing orders, can be used to predict GDP of the present period as early as possible.

There has been a lot of nowcasting practice in current economic forecasting and analysis. For example, Banbura used monthly or weekly indexes of 26 industries to make judgments on current GDP and predict future GDP growth rate and inflation rate.[2] Varian and Choi predicted the present with Google Trends. By taking weekly or daily search data, they analyzed and predicted real-time industrial development and forecast future economic trends.[3] The Business Development Industry and Commerce Index, released by the State Administration for Industry and Commerce (SAIC) of China in 2013, includes ten leading indicators of macroeconomics to predict trends one or two quarters in advance.[4] Economic nowcasting based on big data application will help decision makers to grasp market dynamics in a timelier manner, prevent possible economic crises

CHAPTER 8

early, and accomplish more effective economic management and regulation.

8.3.2 Support mass customization

People's demand for products and services has become more refined, individualized, and diversified with continuous economic development. The supply of large-scale standardized products in the past can no longer meet ever-changing social needs. It's in this context that mass customization emerges. Relying on modern information, new material, and flexible manufacturing technology, mass customization caters to individualized and refined market demands by transforming all or part of product customization into mass production. It serves diversified market entities with low-cost and high-efficiency outputs, and further drives the reconstruction of product structure and manufacturing processes.[5] According to product forms, mass customization includes the creation of products that meet specific needs of customers across the board, such as online transparent customization like AdWords and AdSense provided by Google and tailor-made clothes using 3D printing; also the provision of standardized samples for product transformation by customers according to specific needs, such as smart lamps manufactured by Lutron, in which customers can easily adjust the lighting effect through a built-in program.[6]

As social development goes beyond mass production and towards high-level on-demand production, mass customization oriented to actual demand becomes commonplace. This requires manufacturers to timely and accurately grasp market demand trends. Manufacturing companies involve enormous structured and unstructured data. Big data technology can be applied to the mining and processing of massive data in products, operations, value chains, and other fields. The production information and data generated by these non-standardized products needs to be collected, processed, and analyzed quickly to better guide production – consumer preferences, personalized customization, and other demand data will trigger changes in relatively closed supply. By realizing data exchange between demand and supply, production and supply will have better access to consumer demand and provide more accurate feedback. Simultaneously, demand-guided production is expected to expand effective and high-end supply while reducing ineffective and low-end supply.

8.3.3 *Promote the transformation and upgrade of industrial structure and social governance*

In addition to manufacturing, the application of big data technology has advanced all walks of life and propelled continuous economic evolution. Big data is the core driving force of this industrial revolution. It is also the main feature of a series of new technologies, such as, artificial intelligence, unmanned technology, quantum information technology and virtual reality.[7] Guided by the big data revolution, industrial integration has gained momentum. The combination of traditional industries and Internet technology has deepened, inspiring diversified development of industrial structure and economic growth. Big data itself gives rise to a series of emerging industries and companies with huge development space. For example, Apple uses big data and cloud computing technology in the precise siting of global flagship stores; Walmart rebuilds and optimizes the supply chain on the basis of data mining; and Amazon, Taobao and other online suppliers provide users with personalized product recommendations by mastering and analyzing massive data.

In addition, big data technology is used extensively in all areas of social governance, and supports areas including new-urbanization system construction, smart medical platform reform, and e-government coordination. For example, Satellite navigation, Internet position registration and smart transportation cards can indicate real-time spatial and temporal distribution and behavior patterns of urban residents at the meso level, fully reflecting the rationality urban layout functions and the use of traffic facilities. Micro-level big data provides decision support for detailed urban planning, community management services, and architectural design.[8] In fields with massive data foundations, such as, medical health, food safety, crime control, smart transportation, and smart tourism, big data technology can not only provide accurate decision support in advance, but also facilitate efficient assessment of decision results to guide the rational flow of social resources with a view to sustainable social and economic development.

8.4   Future Opportunities and Challenges

In summary, big data can solve the problem of market information asymmetry inherited from the planned economy period. It enables nowcasting for economic analysis and market management to be more effective. Therefore, in the stage of precise supply management, the new operation mode of market economy that allocates resources by means of planning is completely viable. Of course, this new mode, which is based on big data technology, not only embodies major opportunities, but also faces a series of new challenges.

First, massive data acquisition involves a lot of work, including both structured quantitative information and unstructured non-quantitative information from texts, pictures, videos and other materials. Currently, traditional data collection has been upgraded to data mining. Data cleaning, retention, processing and extraction, as well as standardized structuring all challenge big data technology.

Second, precise supply management requires authentic data sources and targeted policy research. However, there is a relative lack of open data sharing platforms for the development of various industries. The availability of data on major industries is a key task of data platform construction for industry forecasting and supply management at the current stage.

Third, big data analysis and processing systems are more vulnerable to attacks due to high data concentration – there are great potential data security risks. In particular, the non-relational database (NoSQL) that underpins big data technology is relatively weak in data maintenance and needs further improvement.

Since the application of big data in economic activities is not yet mature, and its use in economic analysis and market management is also young, big data cannot completely replace traditional methods of economic analysis. However, with its continuous development, precise supply management based on big data revolution will inevitably rise, enhancing the means of social progress and sustainable economic development.

Endnotes

1. Liu Taoxiong, Xu Xiaofei. Overview of Research on Big Data and Macroeconomic Analysis [J]. Foreign Theoretical Developments, 2015 (1): 57–64.

2. Banbura, M., Giannone D., Reichlin L. Nowcasting [R]. European Central Bank Working Paper Series, No.1275, December, 2010.

3. Varian, Hal R. and Choi, H. Predicting the Present with Google Trends [EB/OL]. http://googleresearch.blogspot.com/2009/04/predicting-present-with-google-trends. html.

4. Task Force of Business Development Industry and Commerce Index of the State Administration for Industry and Commerce. Building the Business Development Industry and Commerce Index based on the Study of Relationship between Enterprise Development and Macroeconomic Development [R]. October 2013.

5. Pine II, B.J., Victor B., Boynton A.C. Making Mass Customization Work [J]. Harvard Business Review, 1993 (9): 108–116.

6. B. Joseph Pine II. Mass Customization: The New Frontier in Business Competition[M]. Boston: Harvard Business School Press, 1992.

7. Chen Qing. Using Big Data to Help Supply-side Structural Reform [N]. Guangming Daily, 2016–12–24 (7).

8. Wu Zhifeng, Chai Yanwei, Dang Anrong, et al. Geography Interacts with Big Data: Dialogue and Reflection [J]. Economic Geography, 2015 (12): 2207–2221.

Chapter 9

Expectation Mechanism: Entrepreneur's Trapezoid

As mentioned earlier, demand is the primary driving force of market. Market imbalance in an imperfect market is essentially a serious deviation between supply and demand expectations. Such deviation may be associated with optimistic estimates of supply that the aggregate demand of existing products exceeds the demand expectations, or the failure of supply to absorb changing demand expectations in product price and utility. Therefore, in some cases of market imbalance, lower prices or installment sales may stimulate the expansion of market demand, but will not expand demand expectations in the market. This only partially alleviates the contradiction between supply and demand by meeting the price decline expectations of some consumers. It does not fundamentally solve asymmetry between supply and demand expectations. For this reason, although market imbalance is unavoidable in an imperfect market, supply expectations need to always keep close track of changes in demand expectations, in order to approach market equilibrium and satisfy demand expectation. In reality, this tracking process is prominently embodied in the gradual mechanism of the entrepreneur's trapezoid, after new products are introduced to the market.

9.1 Two Pillars of Demand Expectations

As mentioned earlier, expectations refer to prejudgments on benefits that can be achieved through next-stage market behavior – demand satisfied or supply realized – made, under the premise of bounded rationality, by individuals and social market players therein formed. Among them, demand expectations include the degree of satisfaction of next-stage consumer utility and the availability of benefits, i.e., utility and benefit expectations – deemed as the two pillars of demand expectations.

Utility expectations refer to consumer expectations of the degree to which goods obtained through next-stage market behavior (purchase) meet their actual functionality needs. Such utility includes practical and preference utility. Practical utility is the life convenience and welfare improvement stemmed from the specific use of goods. Where the demand side is the producer and the needed goods is the means of production, these life convenience and welfare improvements will become favorable factors in the production process. Preference utility is the degree of satisfaction of preferences increased by the purchase of goods. For example, purchasing handbags of high-end brands such as Gucci and LV not only serves the needs of consumers to pack cash, bank cards, portable cosmetics, and other carry-on items, but also meets the demand for psychological comfort and pleasure, including visual enjoyment presented by the design of famous brands, class self-identification brought by the conspicuous consumption of famous brands, and even the satisfaction of vanity.

Benefit expectations are the consumer expectations of consumers to spend less to obtain the above-mentioned practical and preference utility of goods. For general goods, price cuts and discounts on the basis of original prices may be regarded as an effective selling method. After all, consumers obtain utility at lower prices than previously required. In some cases, a commodity has moderate material costs, but very high preference value, so consumers consider it worthwhile and even profitable when paying a high price. The benefit expectation of commodities such as calligraphy, paintings, and art sculptures often fall into this category. In contrast, demand expectations about some commodities still expand in spite of price rises. For example, housing stimulates demand expansion out of utility expectation and/or benefit expectation. If consumers believe in the long-term rise in housing prices, then from utility expectation, now is the best time to get the lowest price for the same utility. If consumers have the intention of investment, then they will make long-term profits no matter when they enter the market (pur-

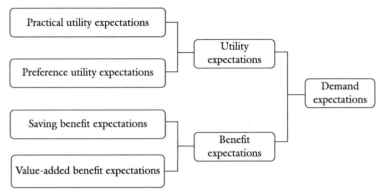

Figure 9–1   Internal composition of demand expectations

chase), and now is the perfect time to reap the greatest profit at the lowest cost.

Utility and benefit expectations are the two pillars of demand expectations. In general, utility expectations have a negative correlation with benefit expectations. In other words, the greater the expected utility, the more willing consumers are to pay more. Vice versa, the lower the expected utility, the more price cuts and discounts are expected to prompt consumption behavior. However, conversely, benefit expectations do not necessarily have a clear correlation with utility expectations. For example, a tulip, the protagonist in the tulip bubble in the Netherlands, as a kind of plant has an expected utility almost the same as other plants such as roses and lilacs. However, when a tulip becomes a speculative object, its price and profit expectations exceed the imagination of practical utility of any plant.

9.2 Supply Expectations and Their Formation

Supply expectations, also known as producer expectations, mainly refer to the profitability expectations about next-stage supply. In the actual market process, they are represented by entrepreneurs. (In early industrial enterprise, business owners as natural persons assumed this role. Later, in joint-stock enterprise the board of directors and the general meeting of shareholders made major decisions, or professional managers entrusted by the board of directors made decisions on their behalf. In the case of individual suppliers such as farmers, producers as natural persons are representative.)

When the supply side notices the emergence of demand expectations and forms a certain social consensus, they will examine the possibility of realization and the degree of profitability to pre-judge whether they can enter the market and make profit. Hereon, three aspects need to be considered:

9.2.1 Degree of technological realization

Demand expectations are derived from desire. People's desire for convenience is boundless, but what can really be satisfied is subject to science and technology they have understood and mastered. For example, transportation tools have always been a perennial pursuit of people. The most convenient tool is surely the flying carpet, but it cannot be realized with current knowledge. Therefore, the second best is pursued.

First, carts driven by animal power such as cows and horses were used. However, this was severely limited in distance (and potentially time). Boats were useful to alleviate these pains to some extent. Owning to technological advancement, transportation tools have changed over time. Steam engines have enabled trains and ships and facilitated long-distance travel. Airplanes, to some extent, have realized people's ideal of the flying carpet. The same is true for other goods. The demand for means of production is also restricted by the degree of scientific and technological realization. At first, steam engines were powered by charcoal but subsequently huge charcoal consumption led to large-scale deforestation in the UK, forcing steam engines to use coal instead.

9.2.2 Profitability relative to cost

When the supply side acquires or possesses certain production technology that can meet social needs, it is necessary to examine the relationship between cost and profitability under this technical system. That is, to evaluate the break-even point. In the initial stage of production, profitability may be not significant. But if such a commodity gains high social popularity, with the expansion of production, cost savings will be likely brought by supply-side economies of scale, proficiency, and division of labor. In other words, future long-term profitability can be anticipated. Such a situation can be seen in almost all industrial product markets.

In some special cases, commodities in shortage may, because of scarcity, reap great benefits for the supply side or rush into related product markets. For example, the Covid-19 epidemic has created huge demand for masks. Without a high threshold for mask production in terms of technical realization, a large number of companies and even manufacturers in automobile and machinery industries quickly switched to mask production. On the one hand, there is significant moral motivation in social concepts. The urgent expansion of mask production can alleviate the tension of social needs in the battle against the epidemic to protect public health. On the other hand, due to enormous social demand for masks, even if the increase in supply suppresses price rises, overall profitability is still great.

9.2.3 Opportunity cost of choice under moral constraints

The supply side needs to confirm demand expectations about a specific commodity (commodity A) and achievable technological conditions for commercialization and certain profit margins. A relatively rational entrepreneur will, before entering the market, examine whether there are other similar opportunities. If other alternatives meet the same conditions – large demand expectations, achievable technologies and greater benefits, the entrepreneur can consider producing another commodity (commodity B) based on the principle of supply expectations aimed at profitability. However, the preference of entrepreneurs, especially the role of moral constraints, cannot be ignored here. For example, some automakers are also engaged in mask production during the epidemic. The demand for cars is also fueled by the epidemic. People are more willing to choose a private mode of transportation due to less risk of virus spread. The demand for public transportation gives way to the demand for private cars, which will inevitably lead to the expansion of

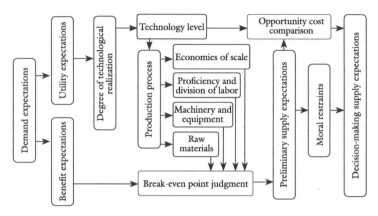

Figure 9–2   Formation of supply expectations

car demand. Moreover, cars present far greater unit profitability than masks. Nevertheless, masks as a necessity of life amid the epidemic far outweigh cars. Out of a sense of social responsibility, some automakers such as BYD have also devoted some energy to the mask market.

9.3   Entrepreneur's Trapezoid

Based on demand information obtained, the supply side forms supply expectations and makes production decisions, which formally gives rise to the new commodity market.

At this time, new commodities cannot often meet the expectations of social needs. As to reason, the demand expectations about new commodities are often just an imagination of practical utility, with form and price unknown. Therefore, the practical utility of the imagined new commodities must be super powerful, while the price is equivalent to or slightly higher than that of substitutes. For example, a horse-drawn carriage is cumbersome, expensive, and difficult to maintain – raising horses, hiring coachmen, and repairing carts, which are all very troublesome. It also lacks private room and requires strict evaluation of coachman quality. The imagined substitute for the carriage should be clean, labor-saving (no need to tidy up stables and clean up manure on the road, and no need to sit behind the horse), and highly private (no coachman needed). While avoiding the troubles of the horse-drawn carriage, the substitute should cost about the same or be acceptably higher.

In other words, the demand expectations about new commodities often include very high expectations about utility and benefit (low price). However, due to the limitation of techno-

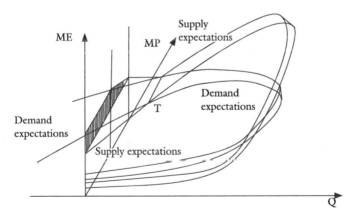

Figure 9–3 Double-wing (utility and price) model decomposition

Source: The figure is drawn by the author.

logical realization and the pursuit of profit by entrepreneurs, the typical expectations of supply are moderate utility and higher price than expected by demand. This creates space between demand and supply expectations, called the entrepreneur's trapezoid, as shown by the shaded area in Figure 9–3.

ME indicates the product utility expectations and MP product price expectations, and Q represents quantity. The upper line of the shaded trapezoid represents demand expectations, including higher-utility expectation and lower-price expectation. The lower line of the shaded trapezoid represents supply expectations, that is, lower utility and higher price at the beginning of supply of new products to market.

With the spatial diffusion of new commodity consumption habits (demonstration effect), social demand is increasing, and so is the scale of production. Product prices will fall for multiple reasons. With the expansion of profit margins, new suppliers will enter the market, giving rise to competition. As a result, both new and old suppliers will be forced to conform to demand expectations and expand research & development investment, so as to make production processes more advanced and continuously enhance product functionality. At point T, both utility and price will be basically consistent with demand expectations. This point is called the singular point of consumption popularity. The process in which the shaded trapezoid shrinks and disappears is the innovation process of entrepreneurs, of which there is no need to go into detail.

After point T, the demand and supply expectations change, as described in the double-wing model. The demand side will continue to expand social consumption in expectations of higher utility and lower price until they are satisfied or notice product drawbacks. Then, they will lose interest, and anticipate new substitutes or new consumer products. The supply side conforms to the downward trend of prices. But in most cases, in order to obtain more profit, they will constantly improve or superimpose product utility and find excuses for high-priced replacements. Of course, this process will have to adapt with demand expectations.

Chapter 10

Expectation Mechanism: Active Supply Management

Under the premise of imperfect market, the market cannot achieve equilibrium. The best state is that supply expectations follow demand expectations as much as possible to minimize wastage. This process cannot be achieved by expanding or weakening demand expectations, but only by means of active supply management.

There are two pathways for supply management: i) spontaneous and conscious management by the supply side; and ii) top-down management by the government. Both are commonly seen in economic activities. Active supply management is the basic micro-condition and most important factor in bringing the market closer to equilibrium.

10.1 Supply Management by Entrepreneurs

Under the premise of imperfect market, entrepreneurs as bounded rational people cannot fully predict aggregate demand and structural upgrade trends. Therefore, they must consciously follow changing demand expectations, and launch new products successively. Only then can it be ensured that supply expectations are infinitely close to demand expectations.

Demand is the most active force in the market. Demand expectations are always pursuing new utility and benefit expectations. Objectively, the supply side is required to continuously innovate and provide new products with lower prices by introducing new technologies, processes, and channels, so as to satisfy changing demand. At the micro level, active supply management by entrepreneurs can maintain innovation vitality and facilitate long-term profitability of companies. At the macro level, it can ensure a rough balance between market supply and demand, reduce the threat of overproduction crisis, and promote innovation as the core driving force.

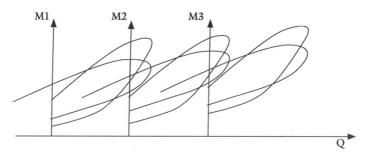

Figure 10-1　Multi-period dual-wing model

As shown in Figure 10–1, M1, M2 and M3 denote the expectations for commodities 1, 2 and 3, respectively, and Q refers to quantity. First, supply follows the demand expectations for commodity 1 to expand production. When the demand expectations for commodity 1 tend to decline, the supply side will promptly pay attention to the emerging demand expectations for commodity 2. It will reduce the investment in production of commodity 1 and turn to the development and marketization of commodity 2, which realizes substitution in market supply. In the same way, the production activities must also be actively transferred from commodity 2 to commodity 3. In actual market activities, there are many cases where demand expectations for product iterations drive supply updates.

Let's take mobile phones as an example. Early mobile phones were just a variant of walkie-talkies that were common in wars. These analog mobile phones supported calling only, had single styles, and weighed too much to be very portable. At this stage, efforts focused on "the loss of weight" of mobile phones. In 1973, Motorola launched phones weighing about 1.13 kg. In 1983, it presented the first commercial mobile phone weighing two pounds (about 0.91 kg) The successor, 9900, launched by the company in the early 1990s was small, lightweight, and durable, but expensive.

Following that, the expectations of personalized needs began to receive attention. Motorola launched the first foldable mobile phone with the same function, opening the prelude to shape personalization. Thereafter, non-English mobile phones, color-screen mobile phones and various brands all became available in response to personalized demand expectations.

With the advancement of technology, mobile phone suppliers have begun to respond to consumer complaints about receiving signals. GSM (Global System for Mobile Communications) mobile phones were costly and more portable, and can receive signals more sensitively with dual-frequency and triple-frequency models. Later, WAP (Wireless Application Protocol) mobile phones came out, opening up the era of mobile Internet.

After teething technical problems were solved, mobile phones began to evolve from simple communication tools to comprehensive information transmission, entertainment, and even office tools. Firstly, mobile games entered the market. With the addition of JAVA extensions, a large number of more vivid and simulated games have been introduced. Secondly, smart-phones appeared and developed larger touch screens, more software, and stronger office functions – eventually becoming life necessities. Later, with the addition of cameras, mobile phones replaced cameras. Meanwhile, it also eliminated the film industry, with the help of electronic storage technology that solves the inconvenience and waste of film in traditional photography. Then, MP3 players and hard disks were added... Now, what we see is a super tool that integrates multiple functions – voice communication; text, sound and image information; transfer and storage; access to the Internet; APPs developed by various information platforms for shopping, studying, chatting, photos and videos, music, messages, and files; and Bluetooth watches to record heartrate, sleep, and exercise.

10.2   Optimism in Supply Expectations

Through the dual-wing model, we can see that supply expectations are always over-optimistic after reaching the singularity of demand expectations, and oversupply occurs. While such a performance-price ratio allows consumers to pay more and still feel worthwhile, compared with practical utility, most of the new and superimposed functions have not been fully utilized. The phenomenon is associated with the greed for profit and innovation inertia of the supply side, as well as the support and connivance of deepening demand expectations.

Generally speaking, demand expectations about ordinary goods start from practical utility. As the supply side responds with new products, products first introduced to the market often have relatively high prices but fail to reach consumer expectations for practical functions. In this regard, consumers continue to express their expectations for practical functions and simultaneously demand a decline in product prices. The demand expectations of low prices become the first problem that supply must solve. Such expectations are eased with the expansion of production scale and advancement of enterprise innovation. The entry of new suppliers in the market increases the choices of goods. As shown in Figure 5–2 in Chapter 5, in order to meet demand expectations, supply strengthens product innovation, and promotes ergonomic commodities that are lightweight and reasonable by reducing redundancy in a progressive manner.

In the above-mentioned process, social demand shows a growing trend in both quantity and structure due to demand expectations of low cost, convenience, personalization and high-quality. As a result, the supply side as a whole makes optimistic estimates beyond demand expectations. On the one hand, this is determined by the fundamental purpose of making profits of supply expectations. As long as the market is expanding overall and the popularity of social consumption has not reached its limit, entrepreneurs will do their best to seek more profits in mature markets. On the other hand, this stems from the inertia of technological innovation. An enterprise's success in developing certain product technology provides the technical foundation for continued development and reserves relevant talents for this enterprise. The technology spillover effects created by peer companies facilitate the virtuous circle of lower-cost and in-depth research & development of related technologies, so the addition and superimposition of features can be achieved.

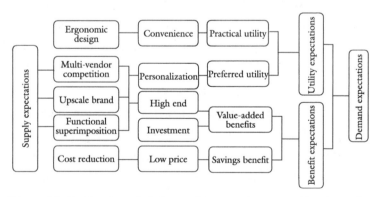

Figure 10–3 Overly optimistic supply expectations caused by demand expectations

10.3 Correction of Supply Expectations

For a long time, entrepreneurs have been unable to overcome the time lag impact when making judgments on the relationship between supply and demand. Economic crises occur typically because entrepreneurs are already powerless to correct overproduction. There are two main reasons behind this phenomenon.

First, traditional market theory that upholds the price mechanism misleads entrepreneurs to making management decisions based on market price. As mentioned earlier, the price mechanism is just a simple summary of human experiences to explain the market operation mechanism. There are serious loopholes in its theoretical logic. Moreover, price cannot accurately reflect the dynamics of market demand and changes in the supply and demand relationship. The price of industrial products generally falls over a long period of time after the introduction of new products. It may be caused by the economies of scale formed as supply expectation expands with demand expectations, or forced by the dull sale of products due to shrinkage of demand expectations.

Second, information acquisition has always been difficult for humans due to information asymmetry and complex social supply and demand dynamics. For this reason, entrepreneurs should be wary of economics based on hypothetical premises. Taking imperfect market as the premise, they should examine expected changes to obtain a more direct insight into the trend of next-stage economic activities. Simultaneously, technological innovation brings huge progress in information acquisition.

With the rapid development of Internet and information technologies, the era of big data has quietly arrived.

The application of big data in economic activities can fundamentally solve the problem of market information asymmetry. Through massive data acquisition, analysis and processing, big data technology enables decision makers to more accurately grasp market demand and allocate resources to fields in real need as reflected in demand expectations, so that on-demand production can be gradually realized. This novel mode of market operation paves the foundation for precise supply management in the new era. It will greatly facilitate real-time tracking and forecasting of market activities, propel mass customization, and guide the transformation and upgrading of industrial structure and social governance, thereby promoting social progress and sustainable economic development.

Chapter 11

Expectation Mechanism: Expectations in the Real Estate Market

The traditional dual-core theory of market economy has become ineffective for explaining new market phenomena in reality. The incompleteness is mainly reflected in the emergence of price failures in large numbers, such as the pan-Giffen commercialization of salt, washing powder, toilet paper, and other daily necessities. In addition, there is a category of most special and most representative goods, namely land property and housing property. In the current prosperous real estate market, price rise has been accompanied by demand expansion. In the case of economic crisis, demand shrinks while price declines.

Furthermore, government activities for real estate market management based on traditional market principles often generate counterproductive effects, due to the limitations of these principles. The more market management ignores expectation trends with bounded rationality, the worse the results. Real estate prices are unnecessarily high, posing huge potential financial risks. This severely restricts the sound development of real estate and endangers national economic security.

11.1 Real Estate Premised on Imperfect Market

The theoretical premise for new market economy principles is the imperfect market. For an imperfect market: i) Economic resources are limited. There is no unlimited supply and demand; ii) Spatial heterogeneity creates obstacles and barriers to market entry for consumers and producers; iii) Products are differentiated and heterogeneous in nature, despite substitutability; and iv) Market information is insufficient and generally asymmetrical. Both consumers and producers have bounded rationality under asymmetric information and their own market expectations.

Clearly, the real estate market is fully consistent with the assumptions of imperfect markets. It is specifically reflected in the following aspects:

First, real estate supply is highly restricted by land supply and price. Especially in China, there are dual imbalances in land supply and land price. In terms of land supply, the national red line of 120 million hectares of farmland must be observed. However, farmland has been reduced by more than 20 million hectares over more than three decades of reform and opening up.

Aggregate land supply will inevitably decrease little by little over time, and urban land use will also be restricted. Land supplied to cities is divided into four parts according to purposes: rural construction, urban infrastructure, industry, and housing. Land really available to consumers is actually very limited. At the same time, urban land disposal becomes tighter and scarcer in larger cities, imposing serious restrictions on supply. Consequently, the larger the city, the higher the land price, which directly leads to the rise of housing prices. In terms of land price, the auction system in the land market will further push it up. In addition, urban reconstruction and resettlement programs in many cities will incur huge land costs. Therefore, the superimposed three mechanisms (auction system, urban reconstruction, and resettlement cycle) will cause high land and rising house prices. In this way, imbalances in land supply and price result in limited supply in the real estate market.

Second, real estate shows serious spatial heterogeneity, manifested in the high degree of regional differentiation caused by supply and demand mismatch. From the demand perspective, differentiation gradually appears among cities of first to fourth tiers. Real estate markets in first and second-tier cities continue to heat up with a sharp decrease of stock, while real estate sales in third and fourth-tier cities slump with considerable stock left over. The differentiation between new houses and second-hand houses is also large. There are more and more obvious differences in supply and demand structure and cyclical changes between real estate markets of different cities or different areas of the same city, and even between products. From the supply perspective, facing an extremely prosperous real estate market, developers never paid attention to the application of new technologies and models. As a result, the single supply structure cannot meet resident demand for upgraded housing or housing quality. The supply market does not innovate to improve quality, efficiency, customization, or community services, which exacerbates regional disparities in the real estate market. In short, the regional differentiation caused by supply and demand mismatch will aggravate regional disparity and impair sustainable growth of the Chinese economy.

Third, real estate as a commodity is highly heterogeneous. Due to land immovability, each house has a unique, unreplaceable position. Houses at different spatial locations enjoy different natural, social, and economic conditions. The style, orientation, floor, scale, decoration, infrastructure and property conditions of buildings also vary widely. These characteristics have strengthened the heterogeneity of real estate, making it a completely differentiated commodity. Moreover, such heterogeneity means that the perfect market necessary for efficient resource allocation does not exist. Real estate is clearly distinct from ordinary goods such as rice, vegetables or minerals.

Most durable goods fall into partly differentiated markets between these two extremes. For example, in the automotive market, cars can be substituted for one another to a certain extent despite various manufacturers and models. In real estate, however, there are no identical properties. Product differentiation implies the existence of monopoly, and product substitutability implies the existence of competition. Where there is differentiation, there is monopoly. The higher the degree of differentiation, the greater the factor of monopoly. Differentiation enables producers to offer diverse products. Therefore, developers virtually all become the monopolist of each property they have developed. With a certain degree of monopoly power, they can decide to some extent housing prices, leading to monopoly price in the market. In particular, real estate products are much more differentiated than many goods in oligopolistic industries. Real estate enterprises involved in monopolistic competition may outnumber those of oligopolistic industries. Nevertheless, the monopoly power of the real estate industry grows strong.

Fourth, there is serious information asymmetry in the real estate market, and both consumers and developers (especially consumers) are rationally bounded. Real estate development generally involves government departments, real estate companies, financial institutions, and consumers. Information asymmetry occurs among these four subjects: i) between real estate developers and consumers. In a seller's market, developers have strong information superiority, including housing location, natural environment, layout and transportation, cost, quality and sales. In contrast, consumers are disadvantaged; ii) between real estate agents and consumers. Real estate agents were originally created to address the information disadvantage of consumers. However, because of inconsistency in interests, consumers are unable to fully grasp information about real estate agents, leading to information asymmetry in the intermediary market. Some agents persuade, for their own interests, the buyer to offer a high price and the seller to offer a low one, so as to earn intermediary charges. A few agents use information superiority to deceive consumers, and make profits by providing low-quality service or housing; and iii) between real estate developers and the government & financial institutions. Real estate developers need government approval for land use and financial institutions to obtain capital investment. Due to constraints in management, professional level, and supervision costs, both government departments and financial institutions find difficulties in acquiring comprehensive information about real estate developers. Also, information asymmetry arises as real estate developers sometimes provide false information for their own interests.

11.2 Dual Attributes of the Real Estate Market

Based on the aforementioned premise of imperfect market, let us look at the special nature of real estate – it has the characteristics of both consumption and investment simultaneously. Real estate is a collective term for land and housing property, in physical and virtual forms: land, buildings and inseparable parts fixed on the land and buildings are physical. The various rights and interests vested in it, such as house ownership and land use right are virtual.

Zhou Jiancheng (2007) believed that with the continuous development of human activities, the attributes of real estate have gradually become multiple, with a transition from necessity to production factors, and further with investment and speculation attributes. By virtue of its natural and socio-economic characteristics, real estate plays a very important role in the entire economy. Its natural characteristics include fixed, finite, and exclusive geographical location; durability in use; finite land resources; and the difference of property services. Its economic characteristics include appreciation, depreciation, and asset-intensive characteristics; bank credit collateral; and investment (value preservation and appreciation functions).

At first, real estate was just a production factor or residential necessity. With the gradual liberalization of financial markets and the improvement of living standards, investment behavior of households and enterprises has become more common. Non-financial assets represented by real estate have risen as important methods and tools of investment. Buyers possess real estate ownership. However, real estate no longer directly participates in the basic activities of production and consumption. Instead, it largely serves investment or even speculative purposes.

For buyers, real estate represents both material and virtual wealth determined by its dual attributes. The house is a physical form of material wealth and an important part of family wealth. In addition, the attribute of speculation (investment) of real estate makes prices highly volatile. Housing prices fluctuate around the real value of houses and are determined by the capitalized pricing method, with certain risks. Therefore, real estate can be considered virtual wealth.

Here, it is necessary to mention two remaining issues. First, is real estate used as an investment or speculative product? Investment behavior is based on the real needs of consumers, while speculative behavior obtains huge profits by buying houses in large quantities. A lot of speculative behavior will create economic bubbles and falsely push up housing prices. This poses huge risks which are not conducive to healthy economic development. The second dispute is whether residential housing is a consumer or investment good. Some Western schools of thoughts upheld the investment theory. Economist Gregory Mankiw also expressed that housing purchases by households and landlords is a residential investment. However, other scholars dispute this. They consider residential properties as consumer goods and necessities instead of investment measures. As they differ from ordinary goods and necessities, their price formation mechanism cannot be derived from that of ordinary goods.

To sum up, real estate is an asset with multiple attributes, including necessity and investment attributes. Since the classification and definition of investment and speculative products is not the research focus here, this thesis only distinguishes the attributes of real estate from the perspective of material and virtual wealth, and categorizes both investment and speculative products as virtual wealth. It emphasizes real estate's dual attributes of consumption and investment or speculation.

11.3 Role of Expectations in the Context of Dual Attributes

As mentioned above, price has always been regarded as the invisible hand in resource allocation, according to classical economics. In actual market behavior, price gradually loses its original directing function, so its capacity to regulate the market becomes increasingly limited. This author believes that Expectations are the fundamental force really determining market operation. Specifically, consumer expectations arouse demand, and then trigger supply through producer expectations. However, this role manifests in different directions and forms under different market conditions.

Let us return to real estate. In this market, the higher the price, the stronger the purchase demand. The craze for real estate has grown in recent years, typically because consumers generally expect prices to rise in future. Such behavior invisibly pushes up market price. Increased returns prompt producers to expect price rises and expand supply. With the increase in supply, the upward trend of prices can be reversed to a certain extent, and demand may be stabilized. However, the attributes of consumer and speculative goods in the real estate market usually transform in this spiral relationship, and the boundaries are often blurred.

From an investment or speculative perspective, real estate is not a daily necessity because it has characteristics similar to financial products. Return on investment is a precondition for the demand side conducting market transactions. The expectations mainly depend on the difference between investment costs and future returns, that is, the difference between future value of real estate and current cost of purchase. Hence, regardless of insufficient or excess supply, as long as demand expects appreciation and can generate more wealth in the future, transactions will happen. In other words, demand expands as price rises. This phenomenon encourages supply to produce an expectation of future revenue increase and then scale up supply. This cycle repeats until demand costs gradually increase to offset the expected returns. By then, price rise will slow down. When a drop in price triggers negative expectations in demand and even supply, both parties will consider a price slump is irretrievable, and real estate owners will sell in large quantities. The lower the price, the smaller the demand. The market will eventually collapse.

11.4   Case Study of China's Real Estate Market

China's real estate prices exhibit a long-term upward trend. Housing price rises were significant especially before 2016, when the Chinese government stated that housing should be for living not speculation.

It is not difficult to see that housing prices have a long-term stable equilibrium relationship with GDP, but there is a short-term promotion relationship. This corroborates that during the ten years from 1998 to 2007, housing prices hiked somewhat after GDP. This decade witnessed high growth rates and realization of vast economic improvements. The upsurge in housing prices injected the fastest and most effective impetus to GDP growth. As long as housing prices climbed, GDP would increase rapidly. In light of such expectations, the government launched several real estate market regulation, monetary and fiscal policies, which have played a role in rapidly pushing up housing prices. In 2007, the financial crisis triggered by the US real estate market came as a global economic shock. It is hard to maintain GDP growth driven by housing prices as the hidden dangers and risks become more apparent. The Chinese economy has evolved and gradually entered a new normal, seeking medium-speed stable growth rather than high-speed growth. With such policy expectations, the real estate policies introduced become more rational and scientific. They no longer blindly pursue market prosperity, but pay more attention to healthy and steady market development.

The price mechanism (of this market) form under the combined effects of sales, land, and leasing. The invisible hand behind this is actually government, consumer, and supplier expectation. China's real estate market is a "policy-backed market" where government regulation can influence the trend more than market regulation. The government first generates expectations about future market trends, and with such expectations, issues related decisions, i.e., macroeconomic and real estate market regulation policies. In line with the government regulation, consumers form market expectations, which also contain considerable sheep-flock effects caused by information asymmetry, and make their own decisions, i.e., buying or selling housing. Changes in consumer behavior will cause demand changes and further price fluctuations in real estate. Upon noticing the price trend, suppliers produce expectations about future returns, and on this basis, determine the method and quantity of future supply. The supply-side changes further affect next-stage expectations

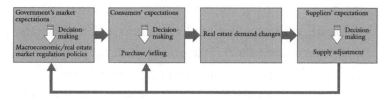

Figure 11-1   Price formation mechanism of real estate market

of government and consumers. The entire real estate market is advancing in this way. The transmission mechanism is shown in Figure 11.1.

The current living-in housing policy advocated by the Chinese government is actually demand-oriented regulation. It can be observed that this is shifting benefit expectations in the housing market. As benefit expectations are gradually replaced by actual utility expectations, the real estate market will return to a reasonable and relatively stable state, step by step.

Chapter 12

Digression:
Why It Has to Be China

China has accomplished remarkable economic achievements since its founding, especially since the reform and opening up that began in the late 1970s. After four decades of hard work, the Chinese economy is on the verge of becoming the world's largest. New technologies and business models are always emerging. With the pioneering application of Internet Plus, new forms of economic activity have sprung up and evolved into new ways of life, such as e-commerce, mobile payments, high-speed rail, and the shared economy. At present, relying on advanced information technology, the decisive role of demand has emerged more clearly. The mass consumption society has moved to a stage of direct involvement in the production process, in which the Expectations of needs for heterogeneity, advancement, and convenience guide and drive the supply-side transformation of production. This new mode of market operation has fundamentally altered the relationship between demand and supply.

So, why is China the first to clearly demonstrate the decisive role of demand in the market economy? Why is China the first to find a true path of demand-oriented supply management to achieve market equilibrium?

12.1 Institutional Advantages

12.1.1 *Regime, System, and Mechanism*

China adopted a socialist system after the completion of socialist transformation in 1956. Although beyond the support of productivity, this system in essence overcame the fundamental contradictions of capitalist production, including the contradiction between the infinite expansion of production and relatively small purchasing power of the people, the contradiction between the organization of individual production and the anarchy of overall social production, and the contradiction between the proletariat and the bourgeoisie. With the establishment of the socialist system, only the first contradiction was left to address, i.e., the contradiction between supply and demand. Production on demand is the core principle of the socialist system.

At that time, China was poor and weak with little industrial foundation due to a century of humiliation amid invasion, oppression and plunder, and civil war. In order to improve people's lives, the new China had to first develop its economy and guarantee supply. Under this system, inevitably demand must be prioritized and supply strengthened to meet demand, which fully conforms to the real operating mechanism of the market economy – demand determines and guides supply.

The socialist system has been sustained by modern China and guided the reform and opening up, leading to huge wealth accumulation. It seems to be contrary to the market economy, but the system is demonstrating institutional dividends most compatible with the market economy. A thorough investigation into the fundamental mechanism of market economy will reveal that the regime, system, and mechanism are not the same.[1] The optimum state of market equilibrium between supply and demand is the ultimate goal, however this is unachievable in an absolute sense.

To this end, it is necessary to accurately grasp demand dynamics and manage the scale and structure of supply based on demand. Planned management is often criticized, not because of the approach itself, but because the technical conditions lag behind the accurate grasp of demand dynamics. On the contrary, the market system lets enterprise independently grasp market dynamics, which cannot avoid excess production, let alone achieve market equilibrium. In the context of market economy, the huge dividend of China's socialist system is reflected in the close attention to demand and effective management of supply.

12.1.2 *Close Attention to Demand*
Attention to human wellbeing is the first institutional advantage

of a socialist system over a capitalist system in the market. The objective of socialism itself is to enrich the material and cultural life of the people. To this end, compared with the capitalist system, it is duty-bound to take demand as the top priority. Before the reform and opening up in 1978, the new China was facing demands both of people's wellbeing and national security, and it built a complete industrial system to this end. However, in the context of the Cold War, coupled with ceaseless hot wars in surrounding areas, the complete planned economic system paid more attention to the needs of national security than those of material and cultural life.

When the tension in the surrounding environment cooled, China embarked on economic reforms, introducing the market mechanism while adhering to the socialist system. This was done with a view to addressing the persistent supply shortage to meet people's needs. Hence, the demand of people's wellbeing has been prioritized. Meeting the needs of more than one billion people has always been the primary concern of the Chinese government. Technological innovation and industrial development are aimed at improving living standards and meeting domestic demand. When some special commodities, such as houses, deviate from the market and give rise to bubbles which threaten economic security, the Chinese government reacts and turns attention to the impact mechanism of consumer expectations. It has been made clear that "houses are built to be inhabited," which suppresses the financialization of housing goods.

12.1.3 Effective Management of Supply

The second institutional advantage that makes the socialist system more suitable for the market lies in the strong control of oversupply.

(1) The state has directly pushed for industrial system construction. In the era of planned economy, through highly efficient supply management, China built a complete industrial system to meet the urgent needs of national security. However, due to the technical constraints of fully planned management, industries meeting the needs of the people's material and cultural life were relatively inadequate. After 1978, China turned back to develop textile and electronics industries to address these basic needs, and further promoted new industries. To this end, some low-profit but indispensable basic industrial sectors were still subject to state-led management under the conditions of market economy. Since then, the Chinese economy has met the basic material and cultural needs of the people, and even shown signs of excessive development. By completely reforming the existing industrial system, it is expected that supply can better match demand.

(2) China's economic planning system, as the product of the planned economy and the market, has played an important role. Economic planning can be regarded as the market-oriented upgrade of China's original economic plan. This was a state-level all-round and unified guideline for national economic activities. Due to constraints in information tech-

nology, it failed to fully grasp national resources and demand dynamics, inevitably deviating from reality in certain aspects. The economic planning covers all levels of the country and the forward planning for industries is represented by the Made in China 2025 strategy.

(3) Under the socialist system, China can concentrate resources on major tasks, providing a powerful guarantee for its rapid rise. When the new China was founded, there was almost no industrial base and everything began mostly from scratch. The socialist system was established to solve the contradiction between an infinitely expanding production capacity and relatively shrinking consumption power of the people on the basis of highly developed capitalist productivity. So then, it must be asked, was the foundation of productivity already in place for the socialist system in China? Were the advanced relations of production compatible with backward productivity in China? The history shows that under China's socialist system the relations of production have exerted a reactionary effect on productivity, thus driving the rapid development of China's economy. This institutional advantage is manifested in the concentration of resources on major tasks. It can be concluded that without this advantage, it is impossible for China to rapidly build its own industrial system and defense power by relying on market accumulation only.

In short, the Chinese economy inherently integrates management of the socialist system. The institutional advantages of this system are true harmony with the internal mechanism of the market economy. Demand in the market is primary and supply is secondary, and market imbalance is inevitable. Therefore, it is necessary to manage supply to meet the demand and further achieve relative market balance. Satisfying the demand is the fundamental mission of socialist construction, and on-demand production is the original intention of the socialist system. Supply management offers an effective way to fulfill the mission.

12.2 Distinct China

China has a long history of cultural and economic development. In terms of industrialization, however, China started late and has then tried to catch up. The late-comer advantages allow China to reflect on the economic theory that guides industrialization, certainly including market principles. The unique soil for verifying and refuting traditional Western economic theory contains resource endowments, such as, vast territory and large population, the special experience of transition from a planned economy to a market economy, and the long-term process of rapid economic growth.

12.2.1 Heterogeneity of Resource Endowments
The heterogeneity of resource endowments is often discussed in the theory of international trade. Under the Heckscher–Ohlin theoretical system, global resource endowments are heterogeneous, but country-specific resource endowments can

often be summed up by one feature. In China, resource endowments show inherent heterogeneity.

(1) In the vast territory of China, there are large differences in topography, landform, climate and resources, and significant product diversity, natural division of space, and regional division of economy. These factors underscore the role of spatial heterogeneity in the market. The heterogeneity of both demand and supply and the limitation of resources all provide sufficient evidence to prove that the premise of traditional market theory – i.e. perfectly competitive markets, is detached from reality. Such a premise implies infinite supply and demand, and barrier-free and even distance-free market entry for producers and consumers.

Spatial heterogeneity brings about the heterogeneity of consumer culture. Some Chinese local products often depend on local consumption habits. For example, millet is a nutrient-rich staple food grown in the Loess Plateau. It has rich iron, protein, calcium, potassium and fiber, and much more vitamin B1 and inorganic salts than rice. The millet soup is reputed to be comparable with ginseng soup. However, millet is hardly needed in southern China and rarely exported to other countries, though China is a big producer and the only producer of millet. This fact proves that demand determines the market and supply cannot create demand. Other examples include lotus seeds, and water chestnuts.

(2) China has a huge population and large market capacity. Particularly since the reform and opening up, along with economic development per capita consumption has surged – from 184 RMB in 1978 to 19,308 RMB in 2015, increasing more than 100 times; and the total population grew from 0.96 to 1.37 billion during the same period, with a net increase of more than 400 million, as shown in Table 12–1. Given a diverse market environment, the huge domestic demand becomes diversified and multi-tiered with the divergence of social classes in the development process. Apparently, it is exactly this diverse and huge demand that provides adequate market support for China's complete industrial system. The dominance of demand over supply has been shown comprehensively in this process.

Table 12–1   Population and Consumption in China

Year	Population (per)	Per capita consumption (USD)*	Urban and rural consumption ratio (rural consumption = 1)
1978	962,590,000	107	2.9
1990	1,143,330,000	174	2.2
2000	1,267,430,000	449	3.7
2010	1,340,091,000	1,613	3.5
2015	1,374,620,000	3,104	2.8

Source: China Statistical Yearbook 2016, http://www.stats.gov.cn/tjsj/ndsj/2016/ indexch.htm.
*calculated in accordance with the exchange rate of current year

At the same time, the structural upgrades of Chinese people's demand have far exceeded the types and structures of supply that the domestic industrial technology system can support. Imports have increased with the help of open-ended information transmission. Consumers become picky about domestic supply and favor foreign products. This further illustrates the choice of supply made by demand – demand upgrade inevitably requires supply upgrade, rather than the idea that "supply creates demand" advocated by traditional Western theory. In the continued process of demand upgrades, supply will inevitably encounter technical stagnation. Moreover, supply is far from capable of "creating demand" in terms of generating the total payment capacity or meeting the Expectations of needs.

12.2.2 External Institutional Effect
China chose the socialist management model of planned economy with the establishment of a socialist system. In the evolution thereafter, this model, influenced by factors outside the system, historically brought about approaches of economic management different from other industrial countries.

(1) China's reform and opening up is a move towards market economy under a planned management structure. For this reason, China cannot give up the model of planned management, to which it has long been adapted. As a matter of fact, China adopted a progressive approach in economic management as well as reform and opening up. This means that a completely laissez-faire model of market economy is

unlikely. In the process of careful exploration, China has taken steps to liberalize the market, and actually benefited from institutional dividends such as close attention to demand and effective management of supply.

In the face of worldwide recession and the huge external impact from accession into the World Trade Organization in 2001, China imposed macro-control based on Keynesian management of effective demand, a doctrine prevalent after World War II. This avoids the re-start from the laissez-faire market and largely prevents the serious "failure" of China's colossal market, thereby demonstrating the necessity and effectiveness of market management. These economic practices make it possible for Chinese economists to reflect on traditional market theory.

(2) Due to the nature of the divided world which came about following World War II (pitting the United States and other Western capitalist nations on one side and socialist states led by the Soviet Union on the other), China has faced economic containment and blockades from the capitalist world since its founding. The Cold War of the 1950s created an "iron curtain" between the socialist and capitalist camps, and ended with the dissolution of the Soviet Union in the 1990s. Nevertheless, the cold-war mentality continues in capitalist countries, as well as the technical blockade against China. Such economic containment further underscores the importance of managed economy. On the one hand, China's large and diverse demand necessitates complete industrial sectors. In the laissez-faire system, contributive

basic industries that are hardly profitable are often not preferred, giving rise to huge supply shortages, while external resources and products are not available due to economic containment. China has to rely on traditional planned management and the power of the state to support these industries. In this sense, external economic blockades and containment maintains, to a certain extent, the necessity of managed economy. On the other hand, after the reform and opening up, the Expectations of needs of the Chinese people gradually aligned with foreign consumption. The new demand has exceeded the supply capacity of domestic industries. To meet the domestic demand upgrade, the Chinese government is forced to develop independent industries, instead of importing in large quantities. In this context, industrial policies are given the means to push forward industrial and technological upgrades on the basis of introducing foreign capital and technology. Herein, the institutional dividends of managed economy are once again reflected. The complete laissez-faire market economy is clearly not suitable for China's national conditions.

12.2.3 Bumping Effect of Rapid Development

China's industrialization development was interrupted by imperialist aggression from countries such as Japan. In the long process of anti-imperialist and anti-feudal struggles, China's national industries developed slowly and the real industrialization process did not unfold until the founding of the PRC. However, it is over this relatively short period of 70 years that China has grown rapidly – from a weak country to a world factory. In the past, industrial products were unable to meet basic needs, but at present, supply has been diversified and become available to the world without compromising self-sufficiency. Especially over the last four decades, China has maintained a rapid annual growth of around 10% and even an annual growth of more than 6% after the global financial crisis of 2008. In terms of economic aggregate, the country is approaching the peak of the world's major powers. Meanwhile, China gradually sharpens its technological advantages in many industries, and contributes most to world economic growth. To summarize, China has taken 70 years to approach a level of industrialization that took almost 300 years for the original industrializing nations, such as the UK and the Netherlands. This shortened process means that China has experienced many of the same contradictions as developed industrial countries, only over a relatively short period. As a result, market contradictions, which are mild and stretched in the long process of industrialization, seem to be intense and concentrated in China's context. Herein, the phenomenon that concentrated market contradictions accompany rapid economic development is called the bumping effect.

Due to the bumping effect, cases that negate the market price mechanism have emerged in a concentrated manner in China. Demand has spurted along with rapid economic growth. It has upgraded from basic physiological needs to rich material needs, and become free from supply restrictions to determine supply in quantity, structure, and even production technology. Demand has always played a fundamental role in China's economic growth. From the perspective of supply, there is a transition from shortage to surplus, mixed with frequent price "failures" and even market "failures."

At the beginning of the reform and opening up, the demand for some commodities increased with price due to inadequate supply immediately after the relaxing of regulations. For example, the demand for soy sauce and salt was greatly boosted by price hikes in the short term. This phenomenon, which does not conform to basic market principles, denotes the consumption choices made by people with bounded rationality under the premise of insufficient supply. During the same period, the price of matches climbed from 0.02 to 0.2 RMB and further to 2 RMB. Such rises did not continue because matches were quickly replaced by simple one-yuan lighters. The supply of matches even lost market significance as the demand structure upgraded with the fast shift to electronic ignition tools for daily use, such as liquefied and fuel gas. Thereafter, for large consumer goods that were once unattainable to the general consumer, such as televisions and automobiles, production expanded with demand, and supply increased despite price decline. This is attributed to the economies of scale in the relevant industries brought by demand expansion. The economies of scale allowed for enough profit, even if the price declined. In this case, demand played a decisive role in supply. These supply changes against price trends represented realistic options maximizing manufacturer profit. In addition, the demand for mung beans, garlic, and ginger also grew with price, due to the rigid demand for subsidiary functions, as well as limited regional supply.

In particular, Giffen goods are commercialized following housing, for which the demand increases with price. There are two reasons behind such phenomena: i) In the face of rising house prices, consumers with rigid demand will choose to buy as long as they are affordable. In anticipation of long-term price rise, it is the best option at the time when market behavior can be realized; and ii) Purchasers aimed at investment would like to buy at any time, in anticipation of a price rise that far exceeds the rise brought by the bank's interest rate and risky stocks. No matter how high the price, purchasers can benefit from buying, and obtain enough returns even by way of mortgage – the interest rate of mortgage is often much lower than that of normal commercial credit. As a result, buyers are not restrained by the soaring house price bubble. In this case, general market principles fail. Demand does not shrink as price rises. Price is no longer the "invisible hand," and it is about to trigger a major crisis that threatens economic security. Other fresh examples in the world include Japan's economic bubble and the subprime mortgage crisis in the United States. The difference exists only in time. China's real estate bubble appeared 70 years after industria-lization began, Japan's economic bubble induced by the property market, 100 years, and the United States subprime mortgage crisis, 150 years.

The above-mentioned cases account for a small portion of the endless market contradictions in China's rapid development process. The concentration of such cases against traditional market principles gives rise to the bumping effect. It does not mean that China is wrong in economic development. It can only show that traditional market principles fail to explain the reality and surely have theoretical limitations and logical errors.

In summary, China's socialist system renders institutional dividends associated with a socialist mode of market management that transcends traditional market principles. The large and diverse needs, the necessary institutional continuity in the reform process, and the external effect of economic blockades by Western industrialized nations, all prove the success of a managed economy. In particular, the bumping effect brought about by rapid development, which concentrates itself within a short time period, has exposed the limitations of classical economic theory, providing fresh evidence for the falsification of the market economy. Though not sufficient to fully illustrate China's economic success, these factors can explain, to some extent, why China challenged the traditional Western theory of market economy earlier. As to China's successful short-term economic catch-up, scholars from the world are expected to provide more comprehensive and thorough analysis from the perspectives of economy, system and culture.

Endnotes

1. Zhao Ruyu, Differentiation and Analysis of Economic Regime, Economic System and Economic Mechanism [J]. Contemporary Economic Research, 1995 (3): 13–16.

Index

ABOUT THE AUTHOR

Ruyu Zhao, Ph.D. in Economics, professor of Jilin University, and Vice President of China National Society of Economic Geography, is an expert in international economics, industrial economics, technical economics, regional economics and general economic theories. He is interested in exploring critically existing economic theories. He speaks at workshops, seminars, and conferences around the world, and has published numerous articles and books. In 2017, he reconsidered the price mechanism of the general market principle, and proposed an expectation-led market principle, which is a new interpretation of the widely-accepted one. His representative works include *An Era of The Wise Man*, etc.